How to Develop
SUCCESSFUL
NEW PRODUCTS

JERRY PATRICK

NTC Business Books
NTC/Contemporary Publishing Company • Lincolnwood, Illinois USA

Library of Congress Cataloging-in-Publication Data

Jerry Patrick.
   How to develop successful new products / Jerry Patrick.
     p.   cm.
   Includes bibliographical references and index.
   ISBN 0-8842-3662-4 (alk. paper)
   1. New products—Marketing.   2. Product management. I. Title.
HF5415.153.P34   1997
658.5'75—dc21   96-39370
                                                  CIP

Published in conjunction with the American Marketing Association,
250 South Wacker Drive, Chicago, Illinois 60606.

Published by NTC Business Books, a division of NTC Publishing Group,
4255 West Touhy Avenue,
Lincolnwood (Chicago), Illinois 60646-1975, U.S.A.
© 1997 by NTC Publishing Group. All rights reserved.
No part of this book may be reproduced, stored in a retrieval system,
or transmitted in any form or by any means,
electronic, mechanical, photocopying, recording or otherwise,
without the prior permission of NTC Publishing Group.
Manufactured in the United States of America.

7 8 9 0 VP 9 8 7 6 5 4 3 2 1

Dedication

*To Susan, without whose help, encouragement,
persistence and aggrandizement, this book
would not have happened.*

CONTENTS

ACKNOWLEDGMENTS

This book was conceived by the innocence of youth on a cold, stormy night in Venice, California. My younger son, Todd, after reviewing my Master's thesis by candlelight, remarked, "Dad, you could be the Carl Sagan of the communication world. Why don't you write a book about your theories?" Being thusly challenged, we finally did it.

And to my son Scott, who provided the encouragement, enthusiasm and personal ambition that set a standard for the entire family, we happily acknowledge his contributions. A successful marketing person in his own field, he learned some good lessons from someone!

There are many others who have made their own contributions to the Perception Expansion Theory through the years; they know who they are, and we are greatly appreciative for their help and guidance. But we would be remiss in not personally acknowledging the help of Ernest Potischman who, through his tenacity, helped us formulate a successful process for new product development.

Kevin Bartelme and Phil Glowatz are highly creative writers who have been very helpful in creating some initial concepts which helped start the processes over the years. Many new products have succeeded largely due to their creative input.

Also to the many clients that have believed in our theory, and have returned for many projects. Among them, Eastman Chemical Company, General Electric, Heineken International, IBM, DuPont, Ore-Ida Foods, and Neutrogena, have made significant contributions.

Finally, a special thanks and acknowledgment for the many contributions of Rich Hagle, Editor, NTC Publishing Group. His persistence, understanding and gentle nudging helped us keep the eye on the ball, and he finally got us to end of the game. This was a trying and tiring process, and worth every minute of it.

Most of all, we hope to make a contribution in reversing the dismal new product failure rate.

INTRODUCTION

Why You Need This Book

This book is the successful culmination of over 30 years of scars obtained on the battlefields of new product development and marketing. It will show you how to dodge the minefields and the marshlands of new product development and marketing.

It reflects on winning battles and on losing battles, but the critical gift is that this book emerges from a learning process taught by all of these experiences and provides a road map for improving our odds of winning. This book examines the lessons of the past to provide enlightenment for successful development of new products in the future.

At the height of a successful career in advertising and marketing, during which he endured years of new product development frustrations, the author returned to academia to try to find a solution to the perplexing problem of why so many new product introductions fail in the marketplace. The failure rate is alarming, well over 90 percent by most estimates, all seemingly good products and services, but torpedoed by the unforgiving consumer.

The author suspected that it was not the technology that was lacking, nor the marketing clout to control the channels of distribution that was causing the high failure rate. Rather, he reasoned that it was a problem of communication, of not matching or properly communicating a product's or service's benefits to the perceived needs of the consumer in a way that motivates purchasing behavior.

By investing the lessons learned in years of marketing experience with advertising agencies, clients, entrepreneurs, and in the academic world, he has learned from the best, and rejected the rest. He has evolved a remarkable process that has resulted in far more successes than failures in new product development. Since refining his new process, he has not had a new product or service that he has developed fail in the marketplace.

1

This book analyzes several new product successes and failures in the light of an innovative process that dramatically improves the success rate of new product introductions. Through these painstaking analyses, and creative application of his marketplace and academic experiences, he presents a clear process for how to develop successful new products.

By carefully analyzing research done by many others, and by augmenting that with his own research, the author found that consumers are often incapable of understanding, and particularly articulating, their true desires, wants, and needs. Consumers often fall victim to their own peers, reference groups, and cultural environments when being questioned about their habits.

This leads marketing executives to base too many of their marketing decisions on research that measures people's *opinions*, which are transitory and misleading. By understanding their underlying *attitudes*, which have been found to be more closely linked with behavior and buying motivation, we can more successfully identify consumers' unfulfilled needs.

Once these attitudes are more clearly understood and linked to behavior motivation, we can then create concepts to satisfy those needs. The author calls this process the Perception Expansion Theory. This book details how to avoid being misled by opinions, how to break the opinion barrier, and how to more accurately identify and analyze attitudes.

Whether you are in top management, looking for shortcuts and more effective methods of developing new products or services, or the executive charged with developing successful new products, or the entrepreneur desiring to capitalize on a hot new idea, this book can help you succeed. Specifically, this book will help you develop and market new products and services by showing you how to:

1. Understand why new product development is the lifeblood of an expanding market-driven economy

2. Understand why there are so many new product marketing failures

3. Identify and avoid the traditional pitfalls to successful new product development

4. Conduct appropriate qualitative research to successfully identify and verify consumers' actionable needs instead of their less reliable transitory needs

5. Modify your product's features and benefits to successfully fulfill the actionable needs of potential consumers

6. Identify emerging trends and corollary needs during this era of rapidly evolving societal changes

7. Avoid the organizational viscosity and constraints that preclude rapid development and marketing of new products and services

8. Understand how real products and services have failed by not using the principles and practices set forth in this book

9. Understand how real products and services have succeeded following the principles set forth in this book

10. Successfully market your own ideas

Why New Product Development Is the Lifeblood of an Expanding Market-Driven Economy

To begin, we analyze why new product development and successful introductions are so important in helping maintain a robust and expanding economy. New products are critical to an organization's growth and to the maintenance of jobs and fiscal responsibility.

Chapter 1 examines why a continuous flow of new product development is important to: help ensure sales growth projections, maintain fiscal responsibilities, keep the organization competitive, spread the marketing risk, lead diversification efforts, keep up with societal changes, capitalize on technical advances, and launch new companies and divisions.

Why New Products Fail

Before we develop a process for successfully creating new products, we take a look at why so many new product and service introductions fail in the marketplace. There are many reasons for these failures, including organizational constraints, inadequate financial resources, management modifications, and so on. The list is almost endless, as marketers have tried for years to find the main cause for marketplace failures.

This book suggests that inadequate, expedient consumer research is the main culprit. From years of analyzing others' marketing research and supplementing that with research of his own, the author has found that most of the failures can be traced to marketing executives accepting research findings that don't identify the real wants, desires, or needs of intended audiences.

While technology has provided new marketing opportunities both for the development of new products and services and for the identification and segmentation of potential consumers, we still have not developed an adequate process for identifying consumers' true needs. We offer them products promising benefits to solve needs they don't have!

Avoiding the Pitfalls to Successful New Product Development

Subsequent chapters of this book show you how to avoid the most common mistakes in new product development and provide a process by which you can successfully create products and services. By following the procedures suggested, and by avoiding some traditional practices that have been in place for too many years, your success rate can be improved dramatically.

Many of the pitfalls are so deeply ensconced in the corporate culture that they cannot be easily changed. But by identifying these problem areas you can more easily find ways to circumvent them, helping to ensure your own success.

In other cases, you can develop new programs that avoid these problems altogether. There are many examples of large organizations that have formed development teams to work outside the corporate structure and that have successfully developed new products, usually in a much shorter time frame than by working within the established framework.

How to Use Appropriate Qualitative Research

Many organizations and entrepreneurs are prone to rely on some of the older, more traditional research methods that have served them in the past. Recent findings indicate that these more easily understood, "safe" methods aren't as reliable or behaviorally analytical as might be expected, thus leading to incomplete or "mis-" information.

However, these are the data available for marketing decisions. Unsuspecting marketing people have followed the indicated actions from this faulty research, and consequently have made decisions that later prove to be marred and lead to marketplace failures.

By understanding why these research programs are inadequate we can structure more appropriate research to identify the opportunities that really exist. Consumers have many unmet needs and desires. It is up to us to properly identify them, and this book suggests a process to accomplish that.

How to Modify Your Product's Features and Benefits to Fulfill the Needs of Your Potential Consumers

We all have desires, wants, and needs. While many of us don't make it a habit of discussing them, or even recognizing them, we have them. Very often we don't fully understand we have the needs until someone offers us something that is appealing to us, thereby triggering a psychological desire to fulfill the need. The key to successful development of new products is to accurately understand those needs that are most often lodged in the subconscious levels of our needs hierarchy.

As marketers, we must identify those needs through appropriate research, then modify the features and benefits of our products to satisfy the needs. All products and services have features, mostly known as *physical* attributes—e.g., fragrance, color, packaging, ingredients. We must be able to convert those features into benefits, which are the *psychological* attributes we rely upon to satisfy our needs.

People satisfy their wants and desires by the psychological gratification provided—the benefits—not by the features of the product or service. Behavior is motivated by the promise of need gratification, which in turn is provided by the benefits we promise through our products and services. Thus, we buy based on benefits; we buy the gratification promised.

Identifying Emerging Trends and Needs

Once we've learned to break the opinion barrier and tap into consumers' attitude levels, we can more properly assess their true needs. This helps us avoid the costly mistakes of developing products and services that are not really needed, only articulated due to peer pressure or the conventions of reference groups.

As technology impacts reference groups, the conventions of those groups tend to evolve into new areas, thus we are left with changing needs. For example, as corporations "right size" and more opportunities open up for home offices, the conventions and the culture of the office reference groups become less important to workers. This has a corollary effect on their needs and consequent needs gratification.

With the process outlined in this book we can more easily identify new and emerging needs through the projective research techniques discussed. As we identify these needs we can determine the new "cultures" that are likely to evolve to provide satisfaction and comfortable surroundings for those needs.

As creative marketers we can then proceed to develop new products and services to ensure that comfort zone and to provide the goods that will successfully fulfill consumers' needs. In return, this provides fulfillment of our needs to maintain a successful new product development program.

Avoid the Organizational Constraints That Hamper New Product Development

Chapter 3 discusses many of the more common organizational constraints that negatively impact new product development. These are the constraints that we often take for granted, the organizational practices that are so common and so widely accepted, based on the corporate culture, that they remain unchallenged. They also remain as potential pitfalls to effective management of marketing development.

While the entrepreneurs reading this may immediately think that these constraints don't affect them, many of them could, and probably do. These are organizational constraints that are so firmly embedded in our business culture that we often process them without even thinking about their potentially negative impact on effective development.

It is quite understandable that someone leaving the structure of a large organization to strike out on his or her own to launch a new product may be very comfortable in using many of the programs and practices learned in the larger culture. If it is good enough for them, it must be good enough for me.

Products and Services Have Failed by Not Using the Procedures Outlined in This Book

Beginning with Chapter 4, and subsequently in each chapter, we will provide examples of products that have failed because they overlooked the procedures discussed in that chapter. These will be actual case studies that illustrate how the developers of the products and/or services should have used the principles presented, but did not, resulting in product failure in the marketplace.

Real Products and Services
That Have Succeeded Using the
Principles Presented

Likewise, we will present actual case studies illustrating how products utilizing the principles presented have succeeded in reaching acceptable financial goals in the marketplace. These are actual products, familiar to most of us, which will be analyzed on the basis of successful needs gratification.

While many factors go into the success or failure of products and services, the examples provided will illustrate how the principles presented were used, and how they added to the success of the products. We don't intend to imply that it was only because these principles were employed that the brands were successful, rather to analyze the product positioning and to indicate how the developers used the principles successfully.

Successfully Market Your Own Ideas

If you are contemplating reaching out on your own to develop and market a new product or service, this book will be an invaluable asset. So many of us have thought or heard about new products that seem to be an ideal solution to a perplexing need.

How many times have we heard someone exclaim that he or she "just got a great idea for a new product" that will make him or her a millionaire? Well, these marketing coups do happen, but not without fighting it out in the trenches and learning to avoid the problems and dilemmas of new product development discussed in this book.

By following these principles, and avoiding the pitfalls mentioned, you can greatly increase your chances for success. So whether you're in top management, wanting to streamline your new product development program, or a corporate executive charged with generating a stream of new products, or the entrepreneur ready to reach out on your own to become a marketing success, read on, and let's explore how to successfully develop new products.

New Products
The Lifeblood of Successful Marketing Growth

"In the next three years alone, about 75 percent of the nation's growth in sales volume can be expected to come from new products, including new brands."

—George Gruenwald

That quote was contained in a survey Booz Allen and Hamilton completed over 20 years ago. But it is probably no less accurate today, as technology is leading an incredible new product development surge and companies continue to place major resources into new product development.

One company the author worked with recently was charged by top management to quadruple sales volume in an eight-year period, most of which had to be generated by new products. Other company executives report having to increase sales by 50 percent in five years, just from new products.

These rates can range even higher in industries where new products are expected on an annual basis, such as cosmetics, fashion, toys, or electronics. Marketing executives accept that new products are essential for growth and to remain competitive in the marketplace.

New Product Development Should Be Consumer Driven, Not Technology Driven

This book takes a decidedly *behavioral* approach to new product development, concentrating on the human factors that affect decision making from the initial product concept, all the way through to purchase decisions made by consumers in the marketplace. As marketers we must understand the consumer needs that motivate buying behavior. These needs, properly identified, indicate opportunities for product development and can lead to successful new products. The technology to develop new products must flow from the needs and must be directed properly to fulfill the needs as they are identified and expressed.

This thesis suggests that there are behavioral considerations within the consuming public that motivate buying decisions and that we, as marketers, must be able to recognize and to understand them in order to successfully develop new products and services. These needs are created and influenced by personal, cultural, and environmental factors. Many are amorphous, others well defined.

Regardless of their source, we must try to identify the real needs and issues, not just the ones articulated by consumers. Those are often misleading, having been influenced by family and peers through reference groups. These needs must be understood by everyone involved in new product development as they must be satisfied by the benefits associated with our product or service. The successful matching of the needs and benefits impact, positively or negatively, the future success or failure of a new product or service.

This concept should not be influenced by existing technology—rather, the proper and accurate identification of people's needs should be the primary objective. In many cases technology must be developed to effectively fulfill the needs once they are understood. This is a reversal of most current thinking, which has led to a conclusion that if we have an exciting new technology, all we have to do is use it to create new products and someone will buy them.

The Need for New Products Varies by Organization

Marketers often fall prey to technology-driven product development due to the omnipresent need for management to develop a stream of new products. The need for new products varies in intensity from one organization to another, but the need is there. There are also many different reasons to have a consistent stream of new products, depending on the goals and objectives of the organization.

Whether the organization markets to a consumer base or has a business-to-business marketing program, there are usually compelling reasons to establish an active new product development process. The reasons for this vary by organization, but usually fall into one of several categories: to help assure sales growth projections, to keep the organization competitive, to spread the marketing risk, to lead diversification efforts, to recognize and capitalize on consumer differences, to capitalize on societal changes, and to capitalize on technical advances.

To Help Assure Sales Growth Projections

Most companies have, as a basic objective, a desire to grow. We don't run businesses to stay in one place. Employees like to have periodical increases in salary, executives enjoy bonuses, and investors in the organization expect to see growth and increasing profits.

Once a company's market share in a given category reaches a plateau, or even begins a decline, executives look for ways to generate additional growth. By creating a steady stream of successful new products we can expect to maintain a positive growth rate and protect the interests of those investors, employees, and suppliers that depend on the organization.

New start-up organizations often experience rapid growth rates in the first year or two, and then fall into the entrepreneurial complacency that growth will continue at the same rapid rate. However, once their market starts to become saturated, those rapid growth rates begin to level in a hurry. This is when new products should have already been developed and readied for marketing to support the growth plan.

As long as companies keep projecting annual sales increases there will probably be a need for new products and services. A few years ago we saw coffee consumption begin to level nationally, and even decline in some markets. But smart marketers developed flavored coffees and gourmet coffees and opened quaint coffee houses to reverse the trend. They found coffee drinkers had a need for a better quality coffee and were willing to pay more for it. The coffee houses provided a social outlet for friends to gather, fulfilling Maslow's belongingness need for these consumers.

CEOs and presidents of organizations won't keep their jobs for long if they do not provide steady growth and profits. This places a major emphasis not only on competitive marketing practices, but also on effective development of new products and services. Some estimates range as high as 25 percent of sales volume being generated from products that have been developed only within the last five years.

To Keep the Organization Competitive

It is highly unusual for an organization not to have competition. There are some companies that become so dominant in a particular category that they discourage competition, but this happy situation usually doesn't last long. IBM was dominant in mainframe computers for several years, but look how that has changed. Volkswagen created and enjoyed dominance in the small car category in the United States for quite some time, and where are they now?

New products are used frequently to keep the organization competitive. Volkswagen didn't generate new products quickly enough and virtually disappeared from the U.S. market until new products could be developed. IBM has had a steady stream of new products in recent years just to remain competitive in the burgeoning computer category.

As needs change and new technologies are developed, opportunities for new products are prevalent. If one organization doesn't capitalize on the opportunities, another one will, and competition is born where none previously existed. Marketing genius and giant Procter and Gamble has long adopted the philosophy that if there is to be competition, let it be within their own organization and try to preempt competitors as much as possible. How many brands of soap does P&G market, or of toothpaste, shampoo, or even of household cleaners?

To Spread the Marketing Risk

Another reason most organizations prefer to focus on new products is to spread the marketing risk among several rather than a few products. The aggressive marketers know not to place "all of their eggs in one basket" and become vulnerable to competitive entries that will dominate and ultimately destroy them. If that happens then there's nothing left, no other brands to develop and mature.

An axiom used by many smaller companies is to never let a single brand account for more than 40 percent of revenues. These companies make it a priority to always be developing new products to avoid the potential dangers of letting one brand dominate their marketing programs and thereby being subject to competitive vulnerabilities.

Some marketing categories are so large that the loss of a few share points can mean incredibly large financial losses, so successful companies maintain a steady stream of new products to spread the risk. In the long distance telephone business, for example, just one share point equates to $1 billion in annual revenues. That's why the marketing dogfight is so critical—neither AT&T, MCI, nor Sprint wants to lose many share points to the competition, and they continually develop new products to spread the marketing risk.

To Lead Diversification Efforts

Many companies establish programs specifically designed to move into marketing segments in which they do not currently have product entries.

By developing or acquiring new products in various other marketing arenas, they can enjoy new growth potential and further spread the risk of losing a dominant brand in a competitive battle.

The successful companies employing this strategy need not diversify outside of their established channels of distribution, but can flex their marketing strength in different categories by utilizing the same channels of distribution. Calvin Klein, for example, has dominated high fashion for both men and women for years, but ultimately began to feel competitive pressures. They then successfully diversified into other categories, but utilized the same channels of distribution—e.g., they began marketing underwear, bedding, jeans, and other garments that could be marketed without opening new routes of distribution.

The Clorox Company has been particularly successful with this strategy. Years ago they were a one-brand company, solidly entrenched in the laundry bleach business, dominant in the category, but with little growth potential from their single product. A new management team adopted a diversification strategy that took them into a variety of new categories, including household cleaners, pet products, insecticides, even specialty foods. They learned very quickly the value of spreading the risk through diversification and growth, and never left the supermarket channels of distribution which they controlled so well.

To Recognize and Capitalize on Consumer Differences

Consumers are by no means all alike. Therefore, it is not realistic to assume that advertising provides a method for selling to the masses. Instead, one must recognize that people of various ages, income levels, and occupations, and from all places and walks of life do not all want the same things, have the same tastes, consume products at the same rate, think the same way or live by the same scale of values. No one [product] is equally appealing to everyone . . . each succeeds best when it is directed to a group of consumers who can be reached on a common meeting ground. (Sandage, et al., p. 125)

It is critical to understand that we cannot and will not sell our products to everyone. It just doesn't work that way. And therein lies a major opportunity for new product development, for if we can recognize the differences in consumer groups, and effectively identify their unfilled needs, this will lead to a successful new product program.

But new products have to be successfully positioned against these target groups. Trout and Reis have literally written the book on product positioning and contend that successful positioning is "an organized system for finding a window" in the consumer's mind. They purport that consumers maintain "ladders" in their heads, the rungs of which are occupied by various competitors in a product or service category. It follows then that we must find our own rungs that nobody else occupies. And this is the importance of proper consumer research and product positioning.

To Capitalize on Societal Changes

Our social order is changing so rapidly these days it is hard to maintain a sense of equilibrium. There are so many factors affecting those changes one's mind boggles at trying to understand them all. However, there are a few that have probably had a more profound effect on new product development than the others:

Time Stretching. With the tremendous number of new opportunities and demands on our time we have a tendency to want to pack more and more activity into each day. We try to *stretch* the time available during a day to accomplish more. The more we can accomplish the better and more satisfied we feel about ourselves.

This necessitates products and services that will help us fulfill this need for accomplishment. While there are perhaps thousands of products that assist us in this quest, there are a few that have become particularly successful, including microwave ovens, food processors, VCRs, answering and FAX machines, cellular telephones, lawn care services, and accounting services.

These products have been hugely successful because they help us save time. The personal computer has not been hugely successful in the home because it does not help us save time. It certainly does in the office, or in a business setting, but not in the home.

The Gray Market. The gray market refers to our aging population base, those aged 50 years and over. As people live longer, and the baby boomers earn more and begin to mature, there is an increasing opportunity for new products and services to satisfy their needs.

As these people get older and have relatively more disposable income than they had as younger adults, their needs change. New needs also emerge, giving rise to new product opportunities such as adult or "retirement" housing, medical care, preventive maintenance health products, travel packages (cruises, tours, etc.), and recreation products (jewelry making, quilting).

Home Office Workers and Telecommuters. Resulting from corporate downsizing in recent years, many ex-employees have found new jobs hard to obtain and have set up offices in their homes. *Home office workers* consist of these people who suddenly find themselves entrepreneurs, or those who take work home with them at night from their regular jobs, or those who moonlight a second job from home.

Also partially as a result of downsizing, but more for the desire to cut costs, many organizations have begun to send employees home to work either full or part time. This group is called *telecommuters*. They are still employed by the organization but work at home on a more or less regular basis.

We are finding that both groups have many needs, not always the same for each group, and marketers are rushing into development to meet the opportunity. Some of these need areas are:

- Consulting services to design efficient home offices

- Ergonomically designed furniture and equipment

- Products for unified power supply

- Services to help employers evaluate telecommuting programs

- Larger monitors

- Products to facilitate communication with corporate offices

- Modular office cubicles

Fitness. When the fitness craze started a few years ago, many marketers dismissed it as a fad. Research, however, kept confirming that it was a continuing trend. The rest is history. Some marketers began developing products that would meet the needs of these new consumers and still be compatible with their marketing and manufacturing expertise.

Those marketers that read the trend correctly have done extremely well. Some of these include bottled water, home exercise equipment, diet plans and products, and light and low-fat foods.

To Capitalize on Technical Advances

Many times new products and services simply fall out of technology advances. It was serendipitous, for example, that a chemist working late one night spilled a new adhesive on a piece of paper. With some frustration he tossed the paper aside and it landed gooey side down, sticking to the work table. A short time later he picked up the paper, noticing it peeled off much more easily and more cleanly than he had expected. He tried it again and, you guessed it, the birth of the popular stick-em notes.

These nice accidents don't happen with great frequency, but when they do the smart marketer must be willing to jump on them quickly. Some synthetic fibers and films have been born this way, leading to the development of very successful consumer and industrial products. While looking for other things, happy accidents can happen, and we must be ready to evaluate them relative to people's needs.

New Products Often Evolve from Existing Products

Repositioning

As brands mature in the marketplace and consumers can readily relate to the intended positioning of a product, the target audiences become well defined and the product's market becomes mature. Consumers drift in and out of the user group as their needs fluctuate, but the growth begins to stagnate.

Smart marketers will seize this opportunity to *reposition* the product—to give it a new definition, or to place it on a different rung on the positioning ladder. Repositioning a brand can give it a whole new life and extend its dominance for many more years. There are some classic examples of brands that have been successfully repositioned, and at least six approaches to repositioning have been used, as described in the following sections.

Repositioning by Attribute. Many new products are actually line extensions, reformulations of the existing products, but are repositioned by introducing a new attribute or feature. This might include a new low-fat margarine, or a sweet butter that introduces a new attribute, or even flavored coffees.

This category would also include basic products that are repositioned without using line extensions, rather just modifying the basic product. These would be the "new and improved" products. Procter and Gamble used this method for years, particularly in the detergent category. They had a successful basic Tide, then there was Tide with enzymes, Tide with bleach, and so forth. It was still Tide, but with new and improved versions.

Repositioning by Price/Quality. Another common way to reposition tired products and services is by increasing or decreasing the quality image, usually supported by price adjustments. Sears, for example, tried to reposition their stores to a higher quality image by introducing designer fashion, higher quality appliances, and other lines.

At first the general public was reluctant to perceive Sears as a higher quality retail outlet, as they were still seen as the catalog store. Cutbacks had to be made and the repositioning appeared headed for disaster. After a series of store closings and financial trimmings the retail giant seems to have survived. Time will tell if they succeeded in increasing their quality positioning.

Repositioning by Use or Application. Many brands and services have been successfully repositioned by finding new uses or applications for them. One of the classic repositionings of this type was for Arm and

Hammer baking soda. For many years baking soda was just that—used for baking. But when the baking patterns began to change dramatically in the 1960s and 1970s and the consumption of baking soda began to drop, Arm and Hammer decided to undertake a major repositioning.

In focus groups and other qualitative research they discovered that many people were using their product as a deodorizer in refrigerators and even to clean teeth and dentures. The product seemed to absorb odors and was very effective at cleaning teeth due to the abrasive texture. Today a major portion of sales is to consumers using the product in refrigerators and freezers to absorb odors. And toothpaste with baking soda is everywhere, even with a major brand of toothpaste by Arm and Hammer.

Another successful repositioning by use is the orange juice story. For years orange juice was consumed as a breakfast beverage. But the Citrus Commission created a successful repositioning to have orange juice perceived as a snack item, or a snack accompaniment. This created an entirely new and large market for orange juice consumption.

Repositioning by Product User. Historically, many products have been marketed successfully to one specific consumer segment. One of the classics has been Johnson and Johnson Baby Shampoo, a good, mild product targeted squarely at babies, who have sensitive skin and eyes.

Several years ago when the birth rate began to drop J&J saw their sales of Baby Shampoo also start down the drain. After conducting some effective qualitative research they discovered that babies aren't the only ones with sensitive skin and eyes. The product was repositioned by product user to reach teenagers and adults with sensitive skin, and sales immediately responded.

Repositioning by Product Class. Occasionally a product has an opportunity to be repositioned by breaking it away from its existing product class and forming a new product category. This was done by L'eggs pantyhose, when they broke away from normal stockings and created a new product class of pantyhose. The automotive industry has utilized this strategy by creating new categories of vehicles, e.g., Chrysler's creation of the minivan, and Subaru's creation of the "sport-utility vehicle."

One of the most successful repositionings by product class is the 7-Up story. For years they fought for recognition against Coke and Pepsi, very successful cola soft drinks. Once 7-Up was repositioned as "the Uncola" the brand took on a whole new definition and had a category to itself. It was the first Uncola to claim to be an uncola, and totally preempted all other non-colas for use of that positioning.

Repositioning versus Competition. Another very effective preemptive strike can be to reposition a brand against its competition. BMW has done this with "The Ultimate Driving Machine," claiming a differentiation and superiority over competition.

But perhaps the classic repositioning versus competition was created by Avis car rental, for years a distant second to giant Hertz. Avis was losing ground and hired a new advertising agency. Doyle Dane Bernbach came up with the classic repositioning against Hertz, "We're only #2 in rent-a-cars, so we have to try harder." There were many executions of the strategy, but that was the basic theme and Avis used it for years. They're still number two, but a lot closer now.

Line Extensions

Line extensions still are probably the most popular and safest way to introduce new products. A line extension is introducing a new product but utilizing the same, albeit modified, brand name. This technique capitalizes on the basic brand's popularity and acceptance, but gives the consumer some options and can result in sales increases for the marketer. The potential danger, of course, is that the line extension could have sufficient product or marketing problems as to damage the franchise of the parent brand.

There are two broad categories for line extensions. The first is where the basic product is improved somehow. The other is where new packaging results in an opportunity for a line extension.

Product Improvement

Product Efficacy. The marketer's dream is when technology allows for a product to be improved in its effectiveness. One of the dangers in introducing "new and improved" versions is that your existing consumer base might feel you've been slighting or lying to them all of those years by selling them an inferior product.

So many marketers have overcome this by simply introducing a new brand, a line extension that has "extra strength," implying a new formulation. There are many examples of this, including Extra Strength Anacin, or Industrial Strength Liquid-Plumr.

Price/Value Relationship. Consumers become familiar with the prices of their favorite products, knowing almost to the penny what they expect to pay. They also develop a perceived value of the product, and have accepted that they must pay that amount for the quality they expect.

One method of introducing line extensions is to change the value perception of the product so that customers must then change the price perception of the product. If you give them more, or something extra, they know they'll be expected to pay more and we can create a successful and more profitable line extension.

There are many examples of this marketing technique, such as when you get extra ounces, or get a contact lens storage kit with your soaking solution. Razor companies often use this for line extension introductions with their offers of buying the improved razor and they will give us "free" blades.

Convenience. We all like to see our favorite products made easier to use, and this is an opportunity for a line extension. If you have a successful brand, but technology delivers you an opportunity to offer your consumer greater convenience, you have a good chance for a successful line extension.

Our pharmaceutical and over-the-counter (OTC) friends do this a lot. Tylenol was a very successful brand, but technology gave them an opportunity for a gelatin capsule, which is supposedly easier to swallow and faster to dissolve. But rather than run the risk of destroying the basic brand by abruptly switching the configuration, Tylenol introduced a successful line extension, Tylenol Gel Caps.

Formulation. Product reformulation leads to many line extension opportunities. As technology or consumer needs change the successful marketer will seize the opportunity to introduce line extensions to fulfill those needs.

Remember when soup was soup? It was probably tomato soup, but maybe chicken noodle. But with innovation and a greater understanding of the consumer, Campbell's has captured a commanding lead in the canned soup business with a brilliant marketing strategy based on line extensions. There's still the regular Campbell's line of tomato and chicken noodle, but now we have Campbell's Chunky, Campbell's Home Cookin', and several others. All were introduced with minimal risk to the basic line and all, we presume, are making handsome contributions to the bottom line.

Packaging

The second major line extension opportunity lies within the area of packaging. Often packaging improvements are driven by technology, but in other cases it is a matter of applying what's already available in a new way that fulfills consumer needs.

Within the packaging category, there are two broad areas that can lead to successful line extensions. Those are in the area of convenience improvements, and in improved performance of packaging:

Convenience. How did we survive our youth without the squeezable ketchup bottle? For years we fought the stubborn ketchup bottle, watched the ketchup race on television—remember when Heinz always lost because theirs was thicker? Then suddenly there was the squeezable bottle that even kids could use. A successful line extension that did not threaten the basic brand franchise, only added to it.

The examples of convenience packaging are endless. Suffice to say that consumers seek convenience, they are willing to pay more for it, and packaging is a good way to give it to them.

Improved Performance. Packaging innovation also provides opportunities for the improved performance of many products. Again, the examples are numerous. The Tetra Brik pouch, for example, was adapted from European technology and used to improve the shelf life and storage opportunities for beverages.

It is amazing that we can buy Irish salmon in vacuum-packed containers that spend days, even weeks in processing and shipping, and yet when we open the package the delicacy tastes only a few hours old, probably fresher than if we had it in a restaurant in Ireland.

So Many Needs, So Little Success

It is well established that businesses must remain competitive, and a steady flow of new products is a major way to stave off competition. With all of these needs for new products, and with all of the technology available today, why do we still have so many new product failures?

In the next chapter we examine the many reasons for new product failures in the marketplace. We look at organizational reasons, the effects of marketplace and competitive activity, even of inappropriate research, technological failures, and many others.

After years of agonizing over this unacceptably high failure rate, the author elected to "go back to the drawing board," quite literally, and to reexamine the communication processes marketers had been using. If the technology was there, and the needs were apparently there, why couldn't we find a match? This had to be a problem of communication. The products were well built, but nobody wanted them. So the author took several years away from the day-to-day corporate world, and returned to academia to try to find some new insights.

After a lot of time in the stacks of libraries and on the computer, the author began to realize that he was on to something. Academic research over the years suggested a behavioral approach was more effective for clear communication, rather than a quantitative or marketplace measurement approach. The marketing methods currently in place just were not giving us effective answers, so he plowed on.

After probably too many hours of reviewing academic and marketing research, plus completing primary research of his own to subject his hypotheses to the scrutiny of real people who have real needs, the author concluded that one major reason for new product failures is inadequate or inappropriate research. For years marketers have been measuring respondents' *opinions* about products and services, and this has been devastatingly misleading for new product development. This method is fine for politics, although often misleading there too, but extremely misleading in determining customers' true needs, which we must accurately identify before we can fulfill them with new products and services.

Chapter 4 presents a completely new behavioral communication model that suggests that customers have a subconscious paradigm for processing data, and that the buying and brand decisions are made at a deeper level than marketers have been acknowledging, or certainly reaching. This paradigm contains a pattern of communication filters through which communication messages, emotional messages, even sales messages, must pass in order to move on to the next level.

As these incoming data are processed, they are matched with other, preexisting perceptions, and evaluated against existing needs that have not been fulfilled. We then form perceptions, opinions, about the new data, and how well they might fulfill those needs. As we form those perceptions, we modify the potential benefits to better fulfill those needs. The author calls this the Perception Expansion Theory, as we try to have the new data fulfill needs that have not been addressed.

For years the marketing community has been content to use marketing research to get an accurate reading of customers' opinions. We read about opinions daily, and review reams of data regarding the importance of opinions. The author's recent findings and experiences, however, suggest that the marketing action is not at the opinion level, but at the next level, the *attitude* level. That's where most buying and brand selection decisions occur, not at the opinion level as previously thought.

What we must do, then, is to break through the opinion level in our research efforts, and try to get to the attitude level. Later, this book suggests methods of doing this, of getting to the attitudes of our customers to discover what their true needs are. Today's customer has built many more filtering processes due to the need to assimilate data more quickly, to set immediate priorities, and to make decisions rapidly.

This suggests that while Maslow's model has worked well for many years, in this new information age, and the resulting information overload, we must reexamine how people process data for need fulfillment. The author's experience to date indicates that the new model presented in Chapter 4 is better suited for marketing success in today's communication explosion.

Maslow's model has provided foresight and guidance through the years. However, we have a different set of problems to deal with, as our customers have had to become more discerning, process data more rapidly, and learn to act more quickly. Chapter 4 gives the Perception Expansion Theory, an entirely new model for communicating with today's customer.

Why New Products Fail

"45,000 packaged goods products were introduced in the United States in the last 15 years! Yet the preponderance of these new market entries were financial failures."

—*Marketing Review*

The extremely high rate of new product failures remains one of the most perplexing problems in the marketing industry. The statistics are truly staggering. Estimates of new product failure rates vary widely, yet most marketing practitioners acknowledge that well over 90 percent of all new products and services introduced each year ultimately fail to reach acceptable sales levels.

While there are no globally reliable statistics on the number and types of new product failures, there are far more new product failures than there are new product successes. And far more new product failures than we should expect, given the recent advances in strategic and production technologies.

Organizations spend millions of dollars a year developing new products and services, and countless hours of management time trying to develop winning combinations of elusive behavioral and scientific factors to ensure marketing success. And yet we still have unbelievably high failure rates.

Also compounding a more precise measurement of new product failures, is the question of what constitutes a failure? Most larger corporations believe a product must generate wholesale sales volumes of $15 to $20 million a year to justify investing high development and marketing costs to get new products into acceptable distribution levels.

Therefore, a larger company may consider a $10 million introduction a failure, but this might be considered a highly successful introduction for a smaller company. New products must generate sufficient sales volume to amortize the development costs over a reasonable period of time, usually within two years, and to make an acceptable contribution to profits over a longer period.

The definition of failure depends on the goals, policies, and objectives of the organization. Smaller clients may be very happy with a "successful" introduction of a line of natural health and beauty aids that generate $5 million in sales after two years. At this projected sales level a larger marketer such as Lever Bros. or Colgate might never have rolled out of test market.

How Do We Define Failure?

In an article in *Marketing Review*, Al Achenbaum gave this definition of new product failure: "[O]f the tens of thousands of new product entries in recent years, only 250, or substantially less than one percent, achieved wholesale sales volume in excess of $15 million, the minimum most companies regard as desirable to maintain an item in distribution."

Al Achenbaum's assessment of a failure rate of over 99 percent not reaching $15 million in sales is undoubtedly directed at the larger corporations attempting to launch products nationally. There are countless smaller companies that very successfully launch brands nationally, regionally, or even locally, with an acceptable sales rate of far less than $15 million.

With the fragmentation of media opportunities in recent years, and the highly focused delivery of cable television messages, we've seen a plethora of successful niche marketing products and services, and very successful regional introductions. For our purposes, therefore, let's define a failure as the inability of a product to reach projected sales levels after a period of two years in the marketplace.

Still, over a 90 percent failure rate is a remarkably negative performance level for a nation with such great global marketing prowess, and with an economy driven by marketing momentum and product and service innovation. The United States currently has over 40,000 professionals employed in marketing and marketing-related positions, has graduated more MBAs than any other nation in recorded history, but we cannot seem to find ways to improve the track record for development and introduction of successful new products.

We have production techniques unmatched by most other countries, and technical research and development that will keep extending the Information Superhighway for many years. Yet for all of our vast resources we are continually unsuccessful in closing the gap between new product successes and failures.

As confirmed in Chapter 1, businesses must continually supply their channels of distribution, and end-users, with new products, new options, new varieties and improved versions of older brands, if only to maintain a share of mind with their important customers and to maintain annual fiscal growth and P&L performance. While there are many reasons why corporations must focus on a steady stream of new products, they are not doing themselves any favors by continuing the same old methods of new product concept development and evaluation. The bottom line is that we must find a way to correct this dismal track record.

According to Lynn Domblaser of *New Product News* in Chicago, over 17,000 new products are introduced each year and, according to Group EFO in Connecticut, upwards of 85 percent will fail. Why? Largely because marketers and even upper management executives continue to trust their own judgment rather than incorporating innovative market research in the development process.

Doubtless, there are numerous rationalizations indulged in board rooms and conference rooms across the country to explain new product failures. Perhaps these "common causes" are often masks used to change the appearance of the real culprit. Too often internal and organizational considerations obscure the real marketplace issues, and effectively circumvent identifying the actionable end-user needs, and the corollary development of opportunities for creating effective new products and services which fulfill those needs.

It has become abundantly clear that most new products fail because management teams, for a variety of reasons, but mostly corporate constraints, are financially motivated to develop the products based on a corporate or manufacturing orientation. They are often rewarded for making maximum utilization of existing corporate technology and resources, thereby minimizing additional capital investment. Thus, the rewards are more often based on maximum utilization of "what is," rather than encouraging reaching outside the existing infrastructure to reengineer the communication and evaluation process.

In other words, it is safer, more comfortable, easier to justify, and often more efficient to make use of existing systems and practices that have been around for years, rather than to develop new, potentially riskier procedures that might generate a higher success rate. With the corporate belt-tightening and "right-sizing" of recent years there is a greater emphasis on the bottom line, and protecting the bottom line often preempts considerations of new and potentially more costly practices, even though these new practices may prove more efficient in the long-term growth of the corporation. The corporate focus often remains on the "now"—meeting profit projections by the end of the quarter or the fiscal year.

This internal or organizational focus reorients management energy into fulfilling corporate issues and maintaining the internal status quo to meet corporate fiscal projections. This shifts the management energies away from the proper marketplace focus of determining the consumers' true unmet needs, then developing products and services to fulfill those needs. Development proceeds at a predetermined pace in line with corporate guidelines and procedures, utilizing existing resources, and without a complete acknowledgment, understanding, or identification of the consumers' underlying needs.

This leads to a lack of a thorough understanding of customer needs, which, when coupled with internal corporate "viscosity," the thickening organizational layers that tend to develop, leads to a management focus on personal growth and survival, rather than gaining recognition and acceptance of the needs that motivate consumer behavior. Corporate internal organizational communication feeds on itself, thereby exacerbating the viscosity, and little innovation is accomplished.

In extreme cases a "closed" system evolves in which the internal organization does not permit energy or fresh input from the outside, as that might disrupt the established protocol or process. When this happens in a closed system, the normal result is for entropy to evolve, and the system is on a road to self-destruction. We have seen many examples of this closed-system process in the business world in recent years, e.g., the down-sizing of IBM, AT&T, and many others.

Our focus is to identify and highlight some of the internal considerations that often contribute to this corporate viscosity, thereby more easily helping to identify potential pitfalls in advance. By carefully examining and correcting these internal constraints we are able to eliminate or correct potential development and marketing mistakes *before the products enter the marketplace.*

Many of these internal considerations contribute to, or are the result of, corporate viscosity and preclude effective new product and service development. In the business world, we often succumb to many internal corporate constraints that prevent our thorough investigation of consumer and marketplace dynamics. These inherent constraints create a corporate culture that is not conducive to doing effective market and consumer research and product development. We "take the eye off the ball" and thereby strike out more often than we hit home runs. Some of these inadvertent constraints are described in the following sections.

Corporate Culture

There is a prevalent attitude among many executives that reflects a form of snobbism, a corporate ego-centrism that reinforces a sense of well-being and "we can't fail" attitude. In its truest form this is an internal, morale-boosting corporate culture that says, for example, "We are experts in our field—we know more about synthetic fibers than anyone else, so how can we fail if we market any products containing synthetic fibers?"

In reality they may know synthetic fibers quite well, but haven't a clue as to how to market disposable diapers, feminine hygiene products, or filtered cigarettes. These are entirely different marketing approaches, fulfilling quite different needs in each category. Just because a company has perfected the development and marketing of synthetic fibers does not give them the knowledge base to market products containing those ingredients, or other products not related to the marketing of synthetic fibers.

This is also true of the company that has developed and successfully marketed a product or service and is now ready to supplement the marketing base with a new product line extension. Xerox learned very quickly that while they were experts in photocopying equipment, this marketing proficiency could not be translated into successfully marketing personal computers.

There is a danger in the entrepreneurial spirit being inflated to the point of myopia that marketing prowess in one category can be translated into other categories. A former client, mentioned above, had successfully marketed a line of environmentally friendly health and beauty aids (HBAs)—e.g., shampoo, soap, body lotions. Because he had established channels of distribution with pharmacies and supermarkets, he concluded that he could successfully extend his line and decided to market a line of health foods.

After several months of developing the products, he called upon his buyer contacts to help launch the line of food products. While he got good initial distribution, trial sales failed to develop. He overlooked the fact that consumer needs for food products were considerably different from the needs for health and beauty aids. His favorable positioning for the HBA category did not translate, in the minds of the consumers, to the food category. The author's consulting firm, Center for Creative Marketing, was called in to correct the problem and after extensive research, a name change, and a repositioning, he was able to successfully extend his line of products.

Just because companies have successfully marketed products in a particular category does not give them carte blanche to successfully market products in a different category. This corporate culture can be devastating in the marketplace, and marketing executives must be careful not to indulge in this cultural complacency.

Organizational Constrictions

All too often the internal structure of a large organization precludes effective and efficient development and marketing of new products. Many times excessive PERT charts and screening committees are formed for self-serving reasons, but actually result in slowing or preventing rapid analysis of changing market conditions, thereby obfuscating the development process.

Many large organizations have a tendency to form new product committees that tend to dilute the creativity and momentum required for effective new product development. One such Corporate New Product Committee (affectionately known as the CNPC) for a major food company consisted of the heads of many departments, including Marketing, Market Research, Research and Development, Home Economics, Distribution, Sales, Finance, Business Development, Institutional Sales, Advertising, Promotion, and Packaging.

This committee was empowered to analyze market conditions, identify marketing opportunities, create new product or service concepts, evaluate the concepts, then produce products and services to match the concepts. Imagine trying to coordinate the schedules of 12 vice presidents just for meetings, while managing an active platform of new product development. Each executive was also motivated by incentive programs to protect his or her own areas of interest, so the turf battles were quite awkward, time consuming, and resulted in very little action. This is an excellent example of corporate viscosity.

Another large food company in the Midwest, at one time, had 18 levels of approvals for new products. Each of these individuals could modify formulas, ingredients, packaging, and so on. Only the 18th person, the president, had the authority for the final approval for the concept; the other 17 could only pass it on or make modifications. This type of structure results in products designed by committee, and often bearing little resemblance to products needed in the marketplace.

Misunderstanding the Consumer Needs Hierarchy

One of the values of benefit segmentation studies is being able to take a fresh look at consumers through a psychographic focus rather than the more traditional demographic evaluations. By understanding the nature of the product or service's psychological positioning, the marketer can understand customers' reasons for taking certain actions—e.g., making purchase decisions.

By identifying consumers' needs, then creating benefit groupings that fulfill those needs, we can measure differences in the groupings, then shifts among them. We can also determine the future makeup of their primary needs. This gives us considerable insight into the types of products and services that will be needed in future years. For too long now, researchers have been content with measuring demographic or quantitative data that give us a "snapshot" at best, a picture of where we are at a given moment in time, but do not predict future trends.

We must realize that individuals are people, not demographics and numbers. We must begin to explore individual consumers as people, as a totality, not just as numbers. These are people with feelings, anxieties, assets, and liabilities. They are people buying products to satisfy individual needs that are not being served by other elements in our society.

When our consumers sense their liabilities outweighing their assets, their real "selves" don't match their ideal selves, and an imbalance exists. They must then take action by initiating particular activities or purchases to bring the relationship back into balance, or congruence. If they don't, some form of incongruence will take over, and discomfort and dissonance follows. But these need shifts belie a simple quantitative or demographic analysis used by most marketers.

Products and services are purchased by consumers to help provide a better balance in their lives. If they have a need for more freedom or escape, they can buy a snowboard or sailboat for temporary congruity or balance. If the need is for esteem, they can find a local dealer to satisfy that need with a new Porsche, BMW, or Mercedes Benz. Importantly, the *individual* can control those activities, whereas jobs, families, and most social relationships are seen as not being controllable by the individual, rather controlled by *peers*.

One eminent psychologist, Abraham Maslow, is noted for his numerous studies in this area. Years ago, Maslow began by studying reasonably well-adjusted people (a novel idea for a psychologist!) to try to understand their particular needs, how they shifted, and how the individuals fulfilled their needs. He then categorized people's needs into five groups, recognizing that individuals could have needs within any of the five groups at any given time.

Maslow found that individuals' needs were omnipresent and appeared with fluctuating intensity depending on various environmental end emotional stimuli. A young baby has a strong need for survival and safety, while a struggling business executive may have a strong need for esteem and recognition. However, if the executive of an advertising agency is fired from her $200,000 a year job, she, too, may suddenly have a primary need for safety and survival. By having an understanding of our consumers' needs and the benefits that will satisfy them, we can be better positioned to predict behavior patterns and consequent purchasing motivation.

Maslow contends that when we explore the needs of consumers, we are exploring the very essence of their lives. It is within this area that he believed we must look at the individual as a totality rather than simply as a demographic element removed from the social structure.

By examining the total human we can identify the emergence of a hierarchy of values which are, again, part of the essence of the individual.

Further, Maslow believed that "These are not only wanted and desired by all human beings, but also needed in the sense that they are necessary to avoid [incongruity and dissonance]."

He further believed that the general motivation theory and particularly the overwhelming desire for need gratification is probably the most significant principle that we, as marketers and new product developers, can study and understand. The predominant factor is the holistic principle that there is a tendency for a new and higher need to emerge as we satisfy current or lower needs. Consumers will always have a desire for new and different products and services to satisfy new and emerging needs, but we must understand their needs and create products to fulfill them.

The gratification of one need does not automatically present a sense of accomplishment or fulfillment. The basic need gratification leads to the emergence of still higher or different needs, and new elements are needed to satisfy those new needs.

Contrary to some interpretations of his theory, Maslow held that it is impractical to believe the basic needs are mutually exclusive and, once satisfied, slip into history. It is highly unlikely that any one desire or need will emerge into consciousness to the exclusion of all others; rather, the individual will experience a series of needs at any one time. These needs will fluctuate, any of them, at one time or another, providing a dominant feeling or desire for gratification, only to give way to yet another need once fulfilled or displaced.

Maslow's basic needs hierarchy begins with physiological and safety needs, then progresses through belongingness and love needs to esteem needs, and the need for self-actualization, which he places at the top of the hierarchy.

The Physiological Needs

The physiological needs are the needs that are usually recognized as the starting point for motivation theory. The very basic desire to stay alive, as well as the needs for food, drink, sleep, warmth, and sexual fulfillment are among these elemental drives. These needs are closely tied to our physical environment, since survival needs are the most basic. The struggle for survival is all that matters to people at this level of the hierarchy.

The Safety Needs

Once the physiological needs are generally satisfied, a new set of needs emerges. These are the needs for protection, whether from social or natural dangers, or even from another human being. Needs found at this level include security, stability, freedom from fear and anxiety, and desire for structure, law, and order. These needs manifest themselves in a common desire for familiar surroundings rather than the unfamiliar. These needs lead to a rather urgent desire for law and order in our society, with a great respect for authority or authority figures.

The Belongingness and Love Needs

If we achieve gratification of most of the physiological and safety needs, a need for love, affection, and belonging will likely emerge. At this level we need the association with friends, a loved one, or children. We crave affection and long for a stable physical setting. The thought of being a part of something larger than ourselves is comforting, to the extent that conformity with a group is appealing. We want to obtain a place in our own culture, and we fear loneliness and rejection, so we seek refuge in our reference groups, religion, and close family affairs. Also prevalent at this level are the concerns and expectations of one's peer groups. "Uniforms," mannerisms, symbols, and group activities are important manifestations of belongingness needs.

The Esteem Needs

Generally, all members of our culture have a desire for a high evaluation of ourselves and seek recognition from others in support of these feelings. These needs may be both (1) for personal strength—e.g., adequacy, achievement, confidence and (2) respect from other people—e.g., status, recognition, attention, and authority. Satisfaction of these needs leads to self-confidence and a strong sense of worth and adequacy. Failure to meet these needs may result in feelings of inferiority and weakness, an overall feeling of not being able to cope with society.

The Need for Self-Actualization

Even if all of the above needs are satisfied, we might expect that a general discontent or restlessness will occur due to our inevitable reach for higher levels of satisfaction. At this fifth level the key value pattern is concern with living up to our inner potential through the full expression of what seems important to us. What a person *can* be, he or she *must* be. We must be true to our own nature. This is our basic desire for self-fulfillment, to actualize our inner potential.

When any hierarchy is presented in a graphic or categorized format, there is a danger that each level will appear independent of the others. This is not the case with our needs hierarchy, and we must keep this in mind for effective needs gratification through new product development.

Most respondents we have studied seem to reflect a similar needs hierarchy, basically in this same relative order. However, life's little disruptions create exceptions to this basic order, as with our advertising executive who becomes jobless on Friday afternoon. Her dominant need for self-esteem, which had sublimated her desire for love, suddenly gave way to a dominant need for survival and safety.

This leads us to the conclusion that the basic needs hierarchy is not a fixed order. We should accept the pattern as a structure in which the individual may flow from one level to another, and perhaps back again to a different level, depending on his or her situation at the moment. This concept has important implications for new product development.

A particular need level need not be totally satisfied, and in fact usually isn't, before the next need begins to emerge. Many people may be partially satisfied in all levels or, perhaps in three of the five, at the same time. However, one of the levels is usually representative of the primary need, and the remaining needs can be represented in declining percentages of importance.

As illustrated in Exhibit 2.1, at any given time a potential new product purchaser may be 80 percent gratified in his or her basic physiological needs, 65 percent satisfied in safety needs, and so on. As a need nears gratification the next higher need may begin to emerge, then the next, and so forth. The critical point to understand is that there is usually not just a single need that the individual is seeking to satisfy, but rather a movement from one need to another with usually only one being dominant at any given time.

It should also be stressed that the needs may be either conscious or unconscious. However, the needs are typically unconscious until some social or cultural action brings them to the conscious level.

One of the more practical applications of Maslow's needs hierarchy for product development is the individuality of the concept. Consider the varying needs of three college professors. Demographic analysis would show them in the same age and income categories, all married with children, and all living in average cost suburban housing. All the same demographically.

However, one professor may be predominantly at the security level and thus focuses on tenure and doing things correctly. Another may focus on increasing his academic stature through research and publications, reflecting the demands of the esteem level. The third may see her task as conveying to her students her own sense of fulfillment from her career, and the beauty and fascination of the world as she lives the self-actualizing life. All three with very different needs, and all candidates for new but very different products and services.

Inappropriate Consumer Targeting

By using Maslow's and other psychographic analyses of potential consumers, it can quickly be seen that the traditional consumer groupings

Exhibit 2.1

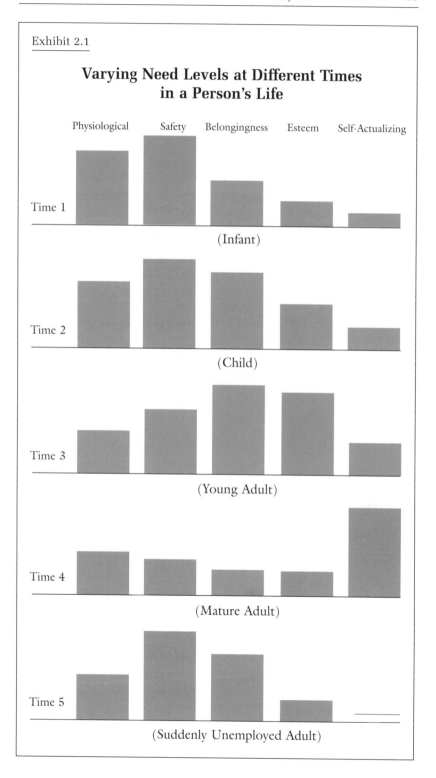

Varying Need Levels at Different Times in a Person's Life

based on demographics are simply inappropriate for today's more complex marketing environment. The fragmentation of media in recent years has led consumers to a far greater diversity of messages in support of their specialized needs. This has supported greater expectations of needs fulfillment due to the enrichment of special interests.

As we develop special interests, and in turn additional needs within those special interests, we seek gratification of those needs to prevent incongruity. Often those new needs exist in the subconscious and are not known or expressed until a particular stimulus reaches them.

By using more appropriate research methods, presented in Chapter 5, we can reach into the subconscious levels and have consumers project their needs. We can then group them by psychographic means rather than the less meaningful demographic methods. By understanding our potential consumers' psychological orientation, we can more easily create new products and services to help them satisfy those needs.

Because of the recent media fragmentation and the corollary development of a greater variety of communication opportunities, our exposure to new concepts is increasing at a rapid rate. This is seen in the plethora of special interest groups, reference groups, even special interest bulletin boards on the Internet. These groups support individuals' needs and expose us to new opportunities for self-fulfillment.

These groups are not defined by a demographic commonality, rather by a psychological or need-driven base. Perhaps this has been the case all along, but as marketers we have persisted in categorizing groups on a demographic basis because the tools to do so are readily available, and it is more efficient. But it is also inappropriate and can lead to a high new product failure rate.

Inappropriate Understanding of Markets

Another popular misconception is not realizing that markets are not analogous—what worked in one market won't necessarily work in another market. Just because you've successfully introduced a new bar soap doesn't give you the expertise to enter the cosmetics market.

Many marketing executives have to guard against the complacency that often results following a successful product introduction, or from the dominance of a particular category. All too often marketers adopt this complacency and a culture of "We're really good, we can do anything correctly," only to find that the next category they enter has entirely different dynamics and requirements unknown to them.

Larger organizations have the luxury of being able to acquire expertise in particular categories. It is common for marketing-oriented companies to hire experts in a particular field, cosmetics for instance, to help research, develop, and market products for that category. But just because you've hit on a seemingly great idea doesn't give you the expertise to develop and market it on your own.

Management Modifications

The "committee effect" can be disastrous for new product development. By the nature of the corporate culture, new product committees will be formed to obtain input from the various departments. Each department is encouraged to "sign off" or approve the product as it makes its rounds through the organization.

Many times products are successfully designed to fulfill consumer needs, only to fall victim to the special interest groups within the corporation. R&D may want the flavor modified to use less expensive ingredients, or Packaging may want a less expensive closure. By the time the product is subjected to all of these variables, it may bear little resemblance to the original design.

But for the sake of expediency, marketers rush the product into test markets, only to see another failure. The modifications changed the product enough that it no longer fully satisfies the consumer needs it was designed to satisfy. Consumers wanted and were willing to pay a little more for that special ingredient, or for that easy-open closure, but management modifications removed it.

Excess Capacity

A popular manufacturing orientation dictates that when you have excess capacity, you create new products to deplete the inventory. Once, a new product development team of which the author was a member was directed by the corporate president to develop a new spaghetti sauce—because we had 16,000 drums of tomato paste in a warehouse in Argentina that we had to get rid of in the next few months. The President explained: "We have a bumper crop of tomatoes and our ketchup and tomato sauce people can't use it all!"

These are the realities of the commodities marketing business, but should these agricultural conditions dictate new product development? To add insult to injury, the team was directed to create a new spaghetti sauce because that's what the President's wife thought we should do. So much for innovative qualitative research.

We had an opportunity to create new products that people needed, but we were directed, because of excess capacity (and a spouse) to create a spaghetti sauce. Later, other firms found an opportunity to use tomato sauce to create flavored sauces, pizza sauces, marinades, and even institutional sauces. But because of the crisis of the moment we were directed to waste millions of dollars on an unsupported hunch.

The By-Product Blues

It is quite normal in the manufacturing and packaging process to have by-products, parts of basic products that don't fit in the end result. This is often the case in processing commodity products such as oils, tomatoes, corn, and fruits. The tendency is to try to utilize as much of the product as possible to minimize waste and maximize profits.

If effective concepts can be developed that make use of the by-products, everyone wins. However, there is a tendency to force-fit concepts just to use by-products for maximum utilization.

At one time, for example, a commodities company tried to use the skins of tomatoes to give salad oil a tomato flavor. The world wasn't ready for tomato-flavored salad oil. Another organization that processed and sold frozen products tried for months to find a use for the surplus skins of onions, to no avail.

Inadequate Technology

It is a difficult thought during these days of rampant technology development, but many products cannot be developed properly because the technology just isn't available yet. Many times marketers have identified needs and developed concepts for products to fulfill those needs, but the technology needed to correctly execute the concepts just wasn't available.

When needs are identified, there is a normal tendency to compromise on the technology and rush the product into the marketplace. The attitude of "Let's get it out there, we'll fix it later" just does not carry in a new product introduction.

Corporate Viscosity

It is particularly difficult to develop new products in what we call "corporate viscosity." This occurs in larger corporations that grow so many management layers and committees that very little can be developed.

A by-product of corporate viscosity is often that top management becomes so insular, a new product concept must grow a "champion"—a person or a team who will push it through the viscosity, making costly compromises along the way.

Consultants are often brought in to help develop new products just to work around the viscosity. Outsiders can usually work more quickly by avoiding the inevitable meetings that tend to slow progress in some organizations.

Conference Room Winners That Become Marketplace Failures

By far the biggest culprit in new product introductions is the management team that believes they already understand all of the end-user needs. These managers are so sure of themselves that they don't spend the time or the resources to find out what the customer really needs.

These are the management teams that come up with new product concepts, pin them on the walls of the conference room, then vote on which concepts they like the best. The winning concept usually gets sent to R&D for prototype development, and the expensive development process has begun.

We call these the "conference room winners," and they're sure to fail in the marketplace, or have to undergo extensive revisions to meet consumer needs. We marketers have a tendency to get too close to our markets, feeling we have the answers and know what the customer wants. If we use flawed research in the beginning, what we know about the customer is also flawed.

Inappropriate Consumer Research

Most new product and service research projects attempt to acknowledge or identify consumer needs, but many of the resulting new products are failing because the systems are built around research designs that provide an inappropriate assessment of consumer needs. These entrenched procedures often inadvertently give misdirection through a process for having target market consumers express *opinions* of options presented to them, rather than for understanding their *attitudes,* which would generate meaningful insights and feedback about their true needs.

Too often we are content with measuring what consumers *say,* rather than digging further to determine what they *mean.*

As explored above, there can be numerous reasons for new product failure in the marketplace, from a poor product concept to poor trade acceptance or heavy competitive activity. However, many product failures can be avoided with proper qualitative research in the early stages.

Too often the corporate culture is so firmly established that we engage in internal practices that have been used over the years without question-

ing or challenging the utility of those practices today. The rapidly changing social agenda of the consuming public has opened new opportunities
for some types of products and services, but has closed or severely modified opportunities for others. Corporate constraints often result in overlooking these changes in favor of maintaining the status quo to assure
maximum utilization of corporate resources, resulting in myopia of marketplace evolution.

It is no wonder that, in many situations, we develop new product concepts internally, without sufficient feedback from, or recognition of significant changes in the marketplace. By continuing to rely on established
research procedures we often miss significant emerging trends that por-
tend new directions in our development efforts.

Many major marketing organizations still labor under the constraints
of committees established to generate, then evaluate, new product concepts. These new product committees are generally charged with creating
products to achieve corporate fiscal goals first, then to modify the concepts as necessary for efficient internal production and cost-saving factors.
The new products survive the internal scrutiny of the new product committees, then are accepted internally as they meet the objectives established (in some cases years earlier) by R&D, finance, production,
distribution, marketing, and sales.

Then we venture into the marketplace looking for verification of executive ideas and conference room winners, rather than having developed
products based on probing our intended target markets to establish concepts that are actually needed. We literally ask targeted consumer groups
to vote on which of our internal, executive concepts they prefer, rather
than first probing to determine the consumers' needs before concepts are
developed. The resulting products are rushed into the marketplace only
to find that while they have survived the scrutiny of the internal new
products committee, they cannot survive the scrutiny of the marketplace
because they meet needs that nobody has.

This preoccupation with dated processes leads to a major misuse of
the qualitative research process, particularly with focus groups. Most
qualitative research practitioners have adopted a similar school of
thought, that focus groups should be used to "focus" respondents' attention on those product attributes developed by the new product development committees. This is the focus groups' task, to verify that those
features presented to the group in concept statements or concept boards
are, indeed, what respondents would expect to find in the products or
services represented.

This is a very typical, and safe, use of the focus group process. It is also
incomplete and misleading.

In a typical focus group, or "focused" interview, the interviewer's task
is to focus the attention of the respondent on certain elements of the concepts and ask very specific questions about those elements. This has been
described by Clement and Grotemeyer (1990) in their work regarding
the role of the focus group moderator:

The task of the moderator throughout the discussions about individual concepts is to find out which of the ideas the (respondents):

- are familiar with;
- like or dislike;
- are interested or not interested in;
- reject and do not believe (why?)
- think might be useful or not useful;
- perceive as new;
- think require more explanation (p. 91)

This typical approach to focus group facilitation in new product development may be effective for verifying corporate predispositions about *corporate management's* concepts, but completely negates the exploratory role of effective focus group utilization for determining respondents' wants, needs, and desires. Importantly to effective product development, attention should not be *focused* on the elements, or on the interest level of the graphic renderings of concept boards. Rather, the primary task should be to have the respondents *explore* and *expand* upon their unfulfilled needs relating to the product category.

The objective of this research step should not be to measure the degree of acceptance of the concepts, but rather to create an environment in which respondents are able to recall, identify, express, or project their needs. Our interest should not be in measuring reactions or counting votes, but rather in helping create products that solve the participants' needs.

To compound the felony, most marketers are content with having end-users "vote" on an array of concepts, selecting one of several that they believe to be the most appealing. In essence, we have been conducting opinion polls among our potential end-users to determine which of a variety of concepts that we have developed is most appealing to them. This is marketing madness, as we are offering them a choice among ideas that *we* like, never mind what *they* like. We have developed a penchant for misusing opinion polls, and we wonder why so many new products and services fail.

CHAPTER 3

Debunking Reality

Socrates and Plato were sitting on a hill one night contemplating the nature of humankind. As dawn occurred, Socrates turned to Plato and said "How beautiful it is to watch the sun rise over the horizon and see a new day beginning. It is one of life's finest moments." To which Plato replied: "But the sun is not rising, my dear friend and mentor, the earth is turning and the sun only appears to be rising."

Given the information, the hard data available to them at the time, who was right? Socrates or Plato? Well, they were both right, because at that time it was not known that the earth revolved. It's a matter of perception, isn't it? From their perceptions of dawn, they were both right. Even today we must deal with individual perceptions and interpretations of given situations.

This simple allegory illustrates that there are no absolute truths in the communication field, only a diversity of perceptions. We all perceive a given situation differently, assimilate our perception into our established framework of similar ideas, and process it as our own—our own truth perhaps, and very different from others' truths who may have witnessed the same event.

Perceptions are motivated by many factors, including the way we assimilate data, our opinions, attitudes, beliefs, and values. All of these subconscious filters influence basic behavior in many diverse ways. We create reality based on our individual perceptions, and those perceptions are filtered by prior experiences relating to similar situations.

One philosopher put it this way:

> Reality cannot exist. Man generates his environment by thinking about it symbolically, rather than merely responding to it or elaborating its input. Our perceptual knowledge is based upon deep conceptual rules of "seeing." We don't store information at all . . . we assimilate it to our ongoing conceptual framework. (Weimer 1978)

A Universal Truth?

It seems to follow, then, that our knowledge of any item or situation, whatever we know of anything, depends on our observation or interpretation of it. Therefore, what we know or can know is only our individual perception of a situation, and others will likely have their own perceptions of it. How then can we ever agree on a "truth" if we define a situation by our individual, personal perceptions? It seems that we create our own truth based on our perceptions, therefore we all have our own truths.

This being so, it must follow that there cannot be a universal truth. In fact, perception becomes reality for each of us. We all have our own individual perceptions and, therefore, our own realities. This presents a multitude of obstacles as we journey through life, as we often assume that other people perceive and understand a situation just as we do, when in fact they have taken away an entirely different perception of it, filtered it differently, and what came out the other end bears little resemblance to what *we* clearly saw and understood.

What a Mess We Make of Communication

This has an overwhelming impact on the communication process. We have accepted communication as:

> The transmission of ideas, emotions, skills, etc., by the use of words, pictures, graphs and other devices. A procedure by which one mind may *affect* another. Communication is a mechanism by which power is exerted, in order to influence behavior.

If the basic purpose of communication is to influence behavior, ideally then we hope to achieve a common understanding between individuals. In essence, we are trying to achieve a transferral of meaning in order to influence behavior in some way. We do this by striving for a symbolic sharing of words, letters, messages, even symbols.

When we set out to introduce and market new products we have assumed a universal sharing of meaning in the words, letters, messages, and symbols we use to influence the behavior of our intended customers and encourage them to buy our services. If we do not fully understand their perceptions of the words and symbols we are using, however, how can we fully communicate the benefits of our products in ways to fulfill their needs? They may have completely different perceptions than we expect when we flash symbols of new products and services that we believe everyone will understand completely.

To develop successful new products and services we see that we must understand and overcome these perceptual barriers. There are specific barriers, outlined in Chapter 4, and there are some more general barriers that can influence our attitudes and values in more subtle ways. These general barriers that influence our opinion and attitude formation, and therefore have a major impact on new product development, include closed systems, monological barriers, ideological barriers, reference groups, and covering laws. They are described in the following section.

Barriers to Shared Perceptions

Closed Systems

A closed system is a communication system that discourages input and influences from outside the system. The internal communication process is carefully designed by the leaders to prevent any communicatio contamination from individuals or institutions not in alignment with their own philosophies.

Closed systems thrive on ritual and on keeping the members closely aligned to the doctrine of the group. These systems can be large or small, but the smaller the group the better the opportunity for the closed system to remain intact.

Many religious groups fall into this category, as they have stringent doctrine that must be accepted and followed to maintain membership. Recruiting of new members is encouraged, expected, and often built in to the ritual. They have their own lexicon when communicating directly, and discourage change and philosophical growth, believing they have already found "truth" and will not be influenced by *outsiders.*

Fraternal and some civic orders are found in this category as well. Many military and paramilitary groups are here, as are many political splinter groups.

Monological Barriers

The monological barrier afflicts those individuals who, as senders of information, are more self-occupied, concentrating on sending their message rather than receiving ours. They pose particular problems for researching new products as they don't really hear our questions and probes, but rather are preparing responses that enhance their own self-esteem.

These are the people who have all the answers, but are not willing to listen to our questions. These are the problem respondents in in-depth interviews—it is difficult to break through the veneer they wear so well. These are the *opinionated* respondents who can be so misleading in new product research. In Chapter 4 we'll explore ways of dealing with them through projective techniques.

Ideological Barriers

Ideological barriers are invoked, usually subconsciously, by individuals who carry strong values. Their values are superimposed on all concepts being explored, and their responses can be very misleading to the researcher who is probing for new ideas and fresh input.

These values may be of a familial nature, religious, political, or any other of a myriad of values we all carry. If, for example, you are doing new product research for a synthetic fiber that will improve the flow rate of cigarette filters, it is a virtual certainty that you will encounter some ideological barriers from strong pro-smokers or anti-smokers along the way. You must find a way around these barriers, or the research will be tainted and you'll be headed for failure.

Reference Groups

Reference groups are the formal or informal collections of people with similar interests or perceptions. These groups provide cues for maintaining cohesion among members, such as uniforms, badges, hats, T-shirts, language, or body language.

Reference groups impact our value structure and, therefore, our behavior. Reference groups consist of human structures from whom we take behavioral cues. These groups provide us with important words, symbols, and emotional charges that are indicators of their mental and value set.

One usually has to join a reference group. Reference groups can be as diverse as a bowling league, or as well-defined as a law enforcement group. There are small reference groups and large ones. The Republican Party, for example, could be considered a large reference group. You have to join it, it has its symbol, the elephant, and it has rules that must be followed to remain a member.

A smaller reference group might be the campus sorority. They have their rituals, they have the symbols, the pins, they have their own lexicon, secret handshakes, all designed to maintain cohesiveness among the members.

If you are trying to reach the members of these groups with new product concepts, you had better determine right away what's driving their attitudes toward your product. Researching at the opinion level will not provide that insight. We must get to the attitude level, because their opinions may be influenced by the reference group. This sort of peer pressure will cause one response because of the group, but once given a chance to express themselves as they really want to do, members will response from the attitude level, unaffected by peer pressure.

Covering Laws

Marketers often encounter covering law barriers in organizations during individual in-depth interviews while developing new products and services for business-to-business clients. If you don't identify these barriers right away, your research can be very misleading.

Covering laws are those implied, sometimes explicit, expectations that are issued from above. They are the rules of an organization that employees learn, very quickly, must be followed. They are seldom challenged, and if they are, usually with dire consequences.

These laws can involve dress codes, the proper way to answer the phone, employee relations, working hours, entertainment practices with other employees, how to deal with vendors, which personal items you may have on your desk, and many other issues. For example, we were told of a marketing professional who had just joined a prominent West Coast company, and the following conversation took place:

> Human resources person: Mr. Sullivan, our hours here are from 7:25 A.M. to 4:35 P.M., and there are really no exceptions to that. If you must work later, by all means feel free to take work home with you.
>
> Sullivan: Those seem to be odd office hours, why are they set at those times?
>
> HR Person: Because many of our employees relied on the train to get to and from work.
>
> Sullivan: But doesn't the train have other stop times?
>
> HR Person: Oh no, Mr. Sullivan. That train hasn't operated in over 15 years.

> Sullivan: But I am not a morning person. I'd be much more productive if I could work from 9:00 A.M. to, say, 6:00 P.M. May I do that?
>
> HR Person: I'm afraid not Mr. Sullivan, but you're certainly welcome to take work home with you at 4:35 P.M.

This is a story. It was related to the author as an example of a covering law that might have outlived its usefulness. However, it is still in place.

Also in place are laws that require machine operators to dress in jackets and ties because it is corporate policy. The author and his associates completed a project recently for a client in the computer services field. We were interested in new product concepts to help ease and expedite installation of networking sites. We spoke with one young man nattily dressed in a beautiful shirt and a designer tie. He was pulling cable for an installation. He apologized for his attire (we were in slacks and sweaters, realizing he would be pulling cable), and said "Ordinarily I'd be dressed in slacks and a sweater so I wouldn't get my tie caught in the equipment, but it is company policy." If you are interviewing these individuals for in-depth new product analysis, you'd better show up in a coat and tie and be out there in the equipment room with them. Otherwise you'll introduce a bias that could skew your findings.

Overcoming the Barriers

It seems that the best we can accomplish is to dig beyond the surface opinions of our target audience respondents, and we do this with our projective techniques. Then we must find similarities among their various perceptions, peeling away the opinions created by the many potential barriers discussed above.

Once we have accomplished that, and we can loosely categorize our respondents into workable target groups, we can then begin to explore the collective needs of those groups. It is critical that we obtain accurate, *unbiased* identification of those needs, or our project fails at this point.

If we can accurately learn what those needs are, then it becomes a matter of creating products or services that offer benefits that will fulfill those needs. At this point we are on the way to successful new product development.

We should point out that up to now we have not dealt with manufacturing capacity, by-products, channels of distribution, or other manufacturing-related concerns. We have put the customers back in the loop, with an orientation toward identifying their true needs, then creating products or services to fulfill them.

This is quite the reverse of the strategy of too many large marketers, who rely on sheer volume, and whose corporate culture says "We are successful, we must know what's best," but who lose 90 percent of their new products.

Features versus Benefits

Once we have accurately identified our customers' needs our task becomes linking our product's benefits, not features, to those needs. There is a very distinct difference between a product's features and the more actionable benefits.

Customers buy products to fulfill needs, and for no other reason. Those needs, or wants, or desires, may be transparent or they may be subconscious, but they are there. There is no reason for anyone to buy our product or service other than because it will help them do something better, more efficiently.

It may make them feel better, or it may help them save time on the packaging line. It may help them save money, or it may help them cut production time thereby increasing overall productivity. But they buy to satisfy a need.

Our customers don't care what color it is, as long as it gets the job done and fulfills a need. They really don't care how many megahertz it has—will it make them look good at the end of the quarter? Show them how they can save money and produce more in the same amount of time, and you've got a sale.

Features are the physical attributes of a product or service, and benefits are the psychological considerations. Customers don't buy products because of the features, they buy because of the perceived benefits, because only benefits can satisfy their needs. A printing press weighing only 1.2 tons, replacing one that weighs 1.4 tons, doesn't satisfy a need, but a press that can double their capacity satisfies a need. If the press is to be installed on unreinforced flooring, however, decreased weight might satisfy a need.

It is critical for us to understand the differences between features and benefits, because customers only buy benefits to satisfy their needs. Here are some examples differentiating between features and the resulting benefits:

Features	Benefits
	Automotive
Anti-lock brake system	Greater safety for me and my family
Dual air bags	Now I can be safe when my spouse is driving

Restraining seats for children	I feel secure that my children are safe

Computers

400 mg hard drive	Plenty of memory storage
Pentium chip	Enough speed to handle my work
CAD/CAM	Help with design and manufacturing

Lighting

High intensity discharge	Greater savings, better lighting
More lumens	Brighter lighting
Fluorescent	Savings

Banking

High yield	Greater income
FDIC insured	My savings are safe
Personal banker	I get more attention, they're protecting me

Beer

Light	Less fattening
Cold brewing	Better flavor
Nonalcoholic	I won't get drunk

With these simple examples we can see the differences between features and benefits. In each of the cases above, it can be seen that customers buy our products and services because of the benefits, not the features. Do you know anyone that tried a new beer because of cold brewing? Of course not. They bought it on the promise of a better flavor. Can you imagine anyone buying commercial lighting because of more lumens? Not a chance, but because they are promised brighter lighting, of course.

Still, many new products are introduced with marketing and advertising campaigns built around features, not benefits. These are the candidates for failures. Here are some examples:

Infiniti: This was not a failure, but a near disaster when the initial campaign sold us rocks, trees, and streams. There was not a mention of what it would do for us or our self-concept. No product-related benefits, not even features.

Personal computers: Introduced with a flurry of megabytes, RAMS, ROMS, all in a language of features. Features that must have meant something to the developers, but nothing to us. Near failure, until they started talking about the benefits—more

Exhibit 3.1

The Unique Selling Proposition Links Features and Benefits to Needs

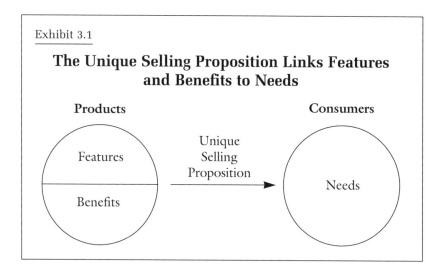

memory, faster calculations, takes up less space. They finally made the language more user friendly.

Anti-lock brake system: The author's firm was retained by an automotive organization to confirm that their introductory campaign was "on target" because they were ready to go. After employing our projective techniques, it was clear that they should not proceed as they had planned, as customers just didn't understand brakes that don't lock, they pulsate. So what? Customers wanted to know the benefits of this, what does it do for them? The campaign was junked, and we now have the anti-lock brake system that offers safety, non-skid stopping, and the other benefits.

Features rarely fill needs. The best axiom is that customers buy benefits, not features. Benefits fill needs. The diagram in Exhibit 3.1 illustrates the relationship between features and benefits, in that usually the features are identified first, during the development process. At that point, however, they must be converted to benefits. Then, if we have properly identified our customers' needs, we link the benefits to those needs.

This linkage is called the *unique selling proposition*, a phrase coined by Rosser Reeves at Ted Bates advertising years ago. The concept is that if we truly have the benefit *needed* by customers, all we have to do is to find a unique way of presenting it to them, a way that appeals to their conscious or subconscious needs, and we'll make a sale. And that's what it's all about.

To do this successfully, however, we must have accurately identified those needs. This takes us back to our basic premise, that we can accurately identify our customers' needs only if we can tap into their attitudes about relevant issues. So let's look at how we do that in Chapter 4.

How to Discover People's True Needs

A few years ago the author went back to school, quite literally, to try to determine what is going wrong in the communication process between the marketer and the end-user that results in such dismal failure rates for new product and service introductions. After several years of academic perambulations, insight began to emerge. If, in fact, we are measuring people's opinions, and that clearly is not working, perhaps we are measuring the wrong factor. Perhaps buying behavior is motivated by something other than *opinions* about a particular topic or product concept.

And, late one night in the University of Southern California library, voila! We found that at least two other communication theorists had completed field studies that started to give us some insights:

> Attitudes have become an important area of study largely because of a widely held belief that they precede the individual's behavior toward the concept. (Tuncalp and Sheth 1985, p. 389)

Interesting. Perhaps people's attitudes toward situations motivate buying behavior, not their opinions. And we've been measuring opinions. So we kept digging, and discovered another interesting finding by a fellow academician:

> One's attitude toward objects is largely determined by the total environment in which he is evaluating the object. (McGuire)

Again, interesting. For decades we have been measuring people's opinions about new products, and using a static environment of typed statements describing the concepts, or open-ended questions asking them to describe an ideal synthetic fiber.

Typically, these concept statements are typed on $3'' \times 5''$ index cards, with no graphics or supporting advertising type copy. A stack of these cards is handed to respondents and they are asked to rank them, from those they like most to those they like least.

A typical concept statement might be:

Surge Protector

- Color coded retractable outlets

- Back-up power

Finally, a way to organize the mess of wires under your desk, and protect your electronic equipment work files at the same time. This new product is a surge protector, provides back-up power, and has retractable cords that keep your wiring organized.

These are static words, attempting to describe a new product concept. Typically, these concept statements have been used for initial screening, and once the research narrows the field, concept boards are completed for the surviving concepts.

There are no visuals, no supporting graphics, no "total environment" in which to evaluate the concept. However, and importantly, since these statements are used for initial screening, it's curious to think about how many good ideas are screened out and lost because there is no total environment in which to evaluate them.

We've been evaluating new product concepts outside of the intended environment and expecting customers to get the full message. If McGuire's findings are at least directional, we've been doing it all wrong.

The Roles of Internal Filters

The more we dug and the more research we completed, the more it appeared that it is not opinions, but attitudes that we should be exploring, and that we should recognize that the environment in which a new product is to be used plays an important role in its evaluation.

In subsequent studies, we tried to find a way to tap into people's attitude level, getting beyond surface opinions, and to put the product concept into an environment that supported, or assisted, his or her evaluation of the concept. But how do we get beyond opinions in an interviewing situation, and is there a difference between opinions and attitudes? Here's our approach:

There are at least five levels of emotions, or feelings, that guide consumer behavior. (See Exhibit 4.1.) These levels, starting from initial exposure to the concept and proceeding through a filtering process that

Exhibit 4.1

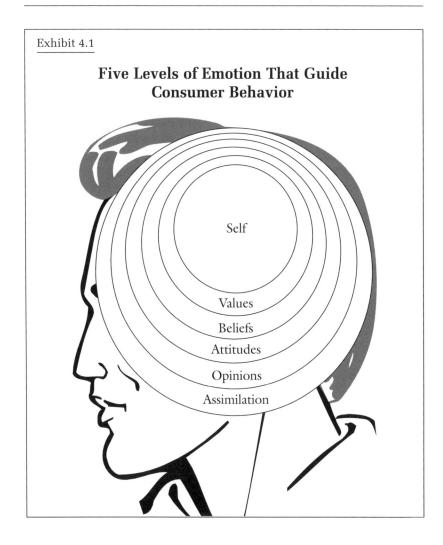

Five Levels of Emotion That Guide Consumer Behavior

ultimately takes us to the *self*, our moniker for the brain power that keeps our bodies functioning, include assimilation, opinions, attitudes, beliefs, and values. Following is a description of each level.

Assimilation

The *assimilation* level represents the first exposure we have to incoming data. These stimuli may be obtained from media, from friends or peer groups, or from our own observations. We are bombarded with thousands of new pieces of data daily (over 2,000 advertising messages alone!) and we must collect them and begin the filing process immediately.

This is the level in which the data are absolutely emotionally clean for us. We have not had a chance to thoroughly process them or to react to them in any emotional way. This is simply our first observation or perception of new information.

As we assimilate new data, we begin to process it, mentally to file it with other similar data previously observed. This is in line with Weimer's contention that we assimilate it to our ongoing conceptual framework.

It is important to understand that we have made no emotional or value judgments regarding the new stimuli. We are collecting it for further evaluation. That evaluation, which begins at the opinion level, may begin immediately, or may be delayed for further evaluation.

Opinions

Opinions are the first emotional responses we associate with incoming stimuli. This is the first time we can say "Hmmm, maybe I like that. I'm not sure (I'll check with my friends and peer groups) but maybe I can like it."

Opinions are the most transitory emotions that we have. We tend to form them quickly, with little forethought. They can leave us in a moment, and are greatly influenced by the environment in which we live. Opinions are changed regularly, they are both influenced and modified by peer groups, by covering laws, and by many other external stimuli.

We refer to this as "bar talk," as opinions are often formed while in the company of others, or our peers, and mostly result from a consensus of the opinions of others. We often form opinions to maintain cohesion within the group. Once away from the group, or placed in another group whose opinions on the same subject may be different, we are likely to change our opinions to maintain the cohesion within the second group.

These are the first indications of potential behavior, but they have not become so entrenched as to motivate our behavior. Our opinions may easily change between the time we leave the cocktail party and the time we get home. We have thousands of opinions, which change regularly, and should not be considered by marketers as a predictor of future behavior.

Attitudes

Attitudes are considered to be general predispositions to respond in a particular way, so to influence and motivate our behavior. This is the first level at which we have found that behavior can be affected.

Fishbein and Ajzen believe that attitudes are "learned tendencies to perceive and act in some consistently favorable or unfavorable manner with regard to a given object or idea, such as a product, service, brand, company, store, or spokesperson" (Fishbein and Ajzen, 1975).

We can now see the importance of understanding attitudes, as each part of this definition is critical for understanding why our customers react as they do toward our services. It becomes critical for us to understand the relationship between attitudes, consumer behavior, and marketing.

Our attitudes are the precursors to the formation of beliefs and values. It is at this level that we process the data and examine it to see how it fits within our value structure. This is the level at which we begin to make decisions about issues and situations, and we become prepared to present those decisions as our own, ready to defend them to the outer world.

We have more intense feelings about our attitudes than we do about our opinions. While opinions are transitory, our attitudes seem to have more staying power. At this stage we have sorted out our ever-changing opinions and now begin a selection process to integrate those attitudes that will help motivate us in future activities.

This is an important step in the motivational process. Once we accept and entrench attitudes toward given situations, filing them with other similar situations as Weimer found, we are saying to ourselves that this fits, this is important enough to keep around to help process incoming stimuli for future use in making decisions.

We also accept that this attitude is not in conflict with any of our beliefs or values. It fits, it is safe, and it is an emotion we can use to get through the decision-making process in a more rapid manner.

It is at this level in the filtering process that we begin to take a serious look at incoming stimuli and make judgments as to whether the new stimuli fits within the structure, and, if it does, whether it can help us in any way. Can it help me solve problems, or feel better about myself, or make me feel more secure? If so, we react positively to the incoming data; if not, the data is rejected.

The attitude level is where we process these data, not the opinion level. If consumers' incoming messages are congruous with their attitudes, or we as marketers can help create positive attitudes, actually tap into that existing bank of attitudes, we have a much better chance of acceptance of our stimuli and congruence is maintained. Subconsciously the consumer says, "O.K. you fit, I will react positively toward you." The sale is made, because we've answered the question "What's in it for me?"

Attitudes might include consumers' feelings toward the deterioration of the earth's environment, how they really feel about the quality of education in their district, or the need they feel to find ways to reduce packaging costs while increasing line speed. People seem to carry between 1,000 and 2,000 attitudes into our daily lives.

Beliefs

Beliefs, and to some extent values, refer to the collective emotions and feelings that we have formed about things and issues. These are the priorities that we set for things. Beliefs are reflected in the way we communicate, through mental and oral statements ("I believe that . . .") and provide cues to our more intense and private values. They reflect a person's particular social and private orientation, his or her knowledge and assessment of something—e.g., another person, a new product, a store, or contemporary social issues.

Beliefs represent still more intense feelings than do our attitudes, but less intense than values. We may have strong beliefs on some issues, but not sufficiently strong to fight to the end for them. Each of us has different beliefs, and they are often in opposition to the beliefs of other family members or peers.

Our beliefs might include the value of higher education, political orientation, or some social issues such as abortion. Psychologists tell us that we normally have between 100 and 200 beliefs.

Values

Values can also be beliefs, and surely incorporate some of the beliefs we have adopted along the way. Values are different from beliefs in that they are more intensely held, we have fewer of them, they are more difficult to change, we don't like to discuss them with others, particularly strangers, and they serve as a game plan for us to maneuver our way through life in a manner that is acceptable to us.

These are the most closely held emotions that we have, including such topics as religion, family, honesty, fidelity, and others. We usually have about 10 to 20 really closely guarded emotions that we've selected, that work for us. We don't like to have these challenged by others; they're ours, not to be disturbed.

These are the most intense of our emotions, and serve as the bulwark of our entire motivational structure, guiding us through the rigors of life. As marketers, we seldom are able to tap into consumers' values. The values are influenced by attitudes and beliefs, but that is as close as we will get to influencing the values of our customers. It is at this level that they say "enough! We'll take it from here."

From this model it becomes very clear that we first begin to form acceptance or rejection of new concepts or new products at the attitude level, not the opinion level. If we cannot find ways of reaching the attitude level, we will continue to measure the wrong emotions and feelings of our customers.

For many years marketers have been conducting opinion polls, thinking we were accurately measuring what people want in new products. All the while we have only been measuring what they tell us they like, at a particular instant in time. But opinions, being transitory, change rapidly, and our data have been misleading.

What happens, in fact, is that as people are exposed to new data that are important to them, the data affect their attitudes. People begin to give the data added importance as they realize the information is congruent with their attitudes. We call this process the *Perception Expansion Theory (P.E.T.)*, because people give new ideas, e.g., new product concepts, additional value as they satisfy their needs. The Perception Expansion Theory proposes that value-added concepts become important to our customers because they perceive that the new products described will satisfy their needs better than the products or services they are currently using. (See Exhibit 4.2.)

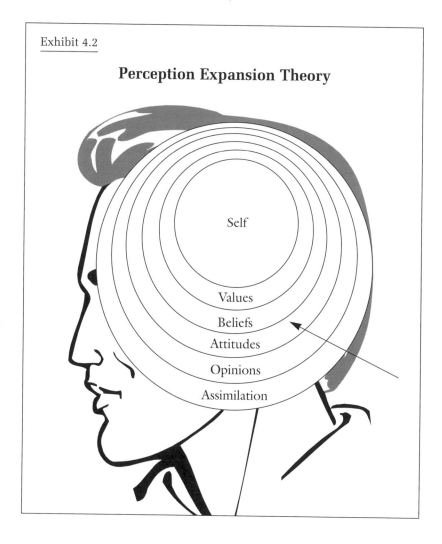

Exhibit 4.2

Perception Expansion Theory

Self

Values

Beliefs

Attitudes

Opinions

Assimilation

Breaking the Opinion Barrier

Because research showed that standard exploratory techniques such as asking respondents to describe an "ideal" product, or polling their opinions, were not appropriate, the author had to develop a new research technique to break through the opinion barrier.

McGuire's findings suggest that a respondent's attitude toward objects (in our case, technology or products) is largely determined by the total environment in which he or she is evaluating the object. In other words, we had to create an artificial environment that would replicate the environment in which consumers would be using the product or service. We had to paint a picture for them so they would be more comfortable, and be able to relate to a familiar situation in which they might use the product.

Our thought was graphically to create an artificial environment that reasonably replicated a situation to which the respondents could relate, in which our new product concept was the hero. Instead of showing customers a typed description of a synthetic fiber, for example, we would show them the potential end result of that fiber in a fabric or a geotextile. We put the product in an end-use situation so they could readily identify with the benefits.

The most effective approach we found was to create concept boards, 11" × 14" graphic renderings suggesting a product-in-use situation. Headlines and body copy presented specific benefits, and, when necessary, supporting copy was attached to help explain complex issues.

As none of our respondents would know anything about the potential benefits of a new technology, we needed to set up the benefits, to provide a stimulus tool to begin the exploratory process. We wanted to create situations with the new technology that were familiar to respondents so they might feel more comfortable about discussing needs or problems which our hypothetical products *did not solve.*

Probing for Negatives

Then we borrowed a page from Rorschach. Go back to your freshman psychology class and recall his famous, and effective, ink blot tests. This famous psychologist developed a projective technique to get beyond his patients' surface opinions. He would show patients a series of ink blots and ask them what they saw in them. Of course objectively, there was nothing there, just a series of black ink blots of different shapes. The patients would then *project* their feelings, attitudes, and needs into the graphic and he would then analyze the results obtained on a deeper, more meaningful level.

This is how we break the opinion barrier. We use the technique proven effective by Rorschach, only updated to the information age. By asking customers to look at the concept boards and give us reactions, they immediately pontificate on their expertise in the area, or tell us how they don't need this. Their first reactions usually come from the opinion level, but we were able to recognize that they must first deal with their opinions (the immediate reactions), and then we probed beyond that.

We get beyond these initial reactions by challenging them on what's wrong with the concepts. We actually probe for negatives, as it is our contention that we learn from rejection. We feel we don't learn anything if we just get agreement; we need to know what the concept *doesn't* solve. In that way, we get respondents discussing, or projecting, their unmet needs. And this is what successful new product development is all about, fulfilling our customers' unmet needs.

Our method paid off: We found that this projective technique was quite appropriate for breaking the opinion barrier, and getting respondents to talk about their attitudes and unfulfilled needs. At times we would actually challenge them to rewrite the headline or the benefit statement to make it more appealing to their situation.

Unfortunately, marketers have developed a fetish for measuring people's transitory opinions rather than their attitudes, where the buying motivation occurs. An example of this is the company that develops several new product concepts, then exposes descriptions of them to groups of end-users. These individuals, typically, are asked to choose which one they like best. Usually, one of the concepts emerges as a clear winner, and R&D is put to work. But has anyone asked the end-users if they really *like* any of the concepts? No, we just asked which of the given group they liked *best*.

This last example accounts for more new product failures than any other reason. As one of our clients said, "For years we've been spending millions of dollars developing products, then hoping that someone needed them!" This just won't work anymore.

From previous experience in developing both consumer and hi-tech or industrial products, we learned how difficult it is, in interviewing situations, to get respondents to describe their needs, or to define or create the ideal product for themselves. Since most respondents cannot create on the spot, if at all, the idea of asking them to "define an ideal application for this new technology" is a useless exercise, although still used by many product development companies.

People buy products and services because of the benefits being promised, not because of features the product may have. Features—product attributes such as color, flavor, and texture—are important, but people buy for one reason only: "What's in it for me?" So we must be able to identify their real needs accurately, before we can create products that offer benefits that fulfill those needs.

Case Study: How Attitudes Affect Product Perceptions

Eastman Chemicals Division, Eastman Kodak Company (ECD), developed and patented a new technology that had the capability of inducing spontaneous wettability into polymer fibers (code named 4SW). The technology has the potential to improve the behavior of a wide variety of products that involve the transfer of fluids—for example, athletic gear, towels, filters.

ECD was desirous of being on the leading edge of new product development, to better serve their customers. Their customers include larger consumer marketing organizations whom ECD supplies with state-of-the-art technology, formulations, and ingredients to manufacture products. Eastman's goal was to provide the latest technology available to help their customers remain competitive.

Center for Creative Marketing (CCM) was retained to explore and identify potential needs and applications for the 4SW technology. The main purpose of the project was to probe beyond customers' surface opinions about the technology, and to identify potential market applications, to prioritize them, and to determine specific product configurations required for each major application.

ECD does not market to the ultimate consumer, or end-user. They market to their own customer base, fabricators or converters who then remarket to the consumers. Therefore, ECD was desirous of assessing the needs of the marketplace to lead the 4SW technology to meet the ECD customers' needs by identifying the end-user needs. For purposes of existing business relations, and for confidentiality, there were certain product categories that CCM was precluded from exploring.

We worked from concept boards—artist's renderings of what the ultimate product may be like—and the respondents had no opportunity to review samples or evaluate technical benefits other than as presented.

The 4SW technology reconfigured the circumference of synthetic fiber to allow it to transfer liquids faster and more efficiently without the need of fiber networks. The fibers were available in several forms, including continuous filament, chopped fibers, single filament, and filament "tows," depending upon the needs of the ECD customers. (See Exhibit 4.3.)

This unique configuration allowed liquids or moisture to be transferred to one end of the fiber, making the fiber usable for a longer period of time, or feeling more dry to anyone coming into contact with the fiber. Swimming suits, for example, would dry faster, or filters would have a longer useful life.

Exhibit 4.3

4SW Cross-Section

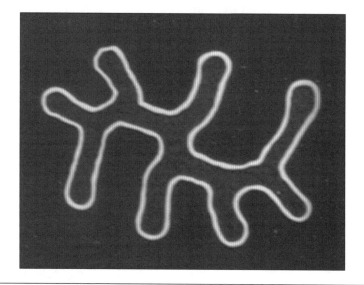

Project Objectives

The primary objective of the project was to explore new ventures and markets for the new spontaneous wettable materials technology, without restriction to product groups, except to exclude certain categories already being serviced by ECD. The assignment was to generate product and service concepts and their marketing strategies that would be appropriate business ventures for ECD, representing appropriate profit and growth guidelines.

The project was to deliver the following information:

1. A list of business opportunities for the new 4SW technology, including estimated market size, product specifications, and price levels

2. A list of key marketing elements including name, positioning, product benefits, and communication elements

3. Potential customers for the new products and services identified during the project

4. Identification of potential licensees for the 4SW materials technology

5. Recommendations for further research and development needed for the 4SW technology

In order to probe beyond ECD's customers' opinions of this new technology, that is, in order to discover any perceptual barriers that might negatively affect their buying behavior, we utilized the projective techniques described earlier. A key to the success of these techniques was our determination to get the customers to talk about the negatives—their needs that our original concepts did not fulfill.

We used concept boards to create a total environment that would offer the "exploratory" group members a variety of more or less provisional product benefits. These benefits were not put together to focus the respondent's attention in the manner of traditional focus groups, where the entire process is meant to separate out the winning concepts from a predetermined list of attributes. The benefits were put into play as prompts: "ink blots" upon which the respondents could project their needs.

As catalysts to a process of exploration and expansion, the concept boards helped to make the respondents active, creative partners in the marketing process. The intention was *not* to determine the final product positioning, which would be left to the ultimate marketers of the products; rather, we wanted to give the technology a marketing definition that was genuinely responsive to the needs of potential buyers. Specifically, we wanted to remove any negatives that might serve as stumbling blocks to successful adoptions, and to discover those positives that could become genuine selling benefits.

To help focus on the determination of these benefits, eight potential product categories were selected and concept boards were created for each of the categories. Those categories were household products, mats and brushes, health care products, textiles, filters, chemical control applications, construction and housing, and geotextiles. A selection of these concept boards is shown in Exhibit 4.4.

Our methodology is covered in-depth elsewhere in the book, particularly in Chapter 13, "Putting It All Together: A Successful Case Study Using the Perception Expansion Theory." In brief, however, we created the initial concept boards on the basis of an initial review of our objectives that was followed by several concept generation sessions, involving staff from CCM and, at times, Eastman. Some of these concepts extended beyond existing technologies, but, in keeping with our philosophy that successful new product concepts can lead to the creation of new technologies, we asked Eastman to let us include these concepts in the process. The concepts generated by this process were then presented in stages, or waves, both to potential marketers and to potential end-users—consumers drawn from specific target markets. The results of each round of exploration with these respondents were analyzed, and the boards changed according to those findings. In many cases, the finalized concept boards bore little resemblance to their first-generation precursors and in other instances had been developed entirely as a consequence of exploratory feedback.

Exhibit   4.4

4SW Concept Boards

Absorbo Provides 50% Quicker Absorbency Than Traditional Wipes.

An Athlete's Footing Is His Fortune...TurfDry Provides It.

With new VEREL liner, floppy disks have less debris ~ last longer

Swim Slicks Lets You Sit Comfortably In A "Wet" Suit.

What's in It for Me?

For several years now, above each desk at the Center for Creative Marketing, we have hung nicely framed reminders, with only the following inscription:

W.I.I.F.M.?

What's in it for me? What is our potential customer really looking for in a new product or service? How will it benefit him or her? What need or desire are we fulfilling with our new product?

This is a continual reminder that we must always find those benefits in new products that will satisfy customers' needs. Nothing else matters. Features don't matter, because customers don't buy features, they only buy benefits that satisfy their needs. Features play an important role, of course, because they deliver the benefits that satisfy the needs. And we must always find those benefits within the features of the product or service that will be most effective in motivating our potential customers to take action.

Understanding how people process data in our new information age leads us to question just how much commonality we can expect among our customers. From the first exposure to a new message, in the assimilation stage, consumers process the new data through a series of filters until they can accept the information as being congruent with previous experiences and existing attitudes, or they reject it as being incongruent with their value systems. Through the entire process they keep examining the new information in terms of "What will this do for me?"

If they reject the new information, the process ends there. If the new data makes it through their filtration systems, it will be filed the way *they have defined it* to make it acceptable. Everyone exposed to the data will invoke the same process, defining it to make it acceptable to them. So if ten people, one hundred, or even a million see a message from us, they will have many different interpretations of that same message. It will be modified, however so slightly, to fit within the communication framework of each individual.

Just as the messages are different, so are the people. Our customers are not all alike, with the same attitudes or value systems. Everyone is different, and our task is to find similarities among them so we can segment them into groups with members having similar needs. Then we can be more proficient in marketing our products and services to them. This is how C. H. Sandage, a dean of advertising theory, sees it:

> Consumers are by no means all alike. Therefore, it is not realistic to assume that advertising provides a method for selling to the masses. Instead, one must recognize that people of various ages, income levels, and occupations, and from all places and walks of life do not all want the same things, have the same tastes, consume products at the same rate, think the same way, or live by the same scale of values. No one advertisement is equally appealing to everyone . . . each advertisement succeeds best when it is directed to a group of consumers who can be reached on a common meeting ground. (Sandage, Fryburger, and Rotzoll 1985, p. 125)

If we must direct our marketing efforts toward groups of people, as Sandage suggests, and we certainly agree, then the process of forming those groups becomes critical. How do we decide upon the criteria for group formation? What is of common importance to a wide variety of individuals that constitutes their selection for a particular group?

Our task becomes one of creating groups, or *segments* of the market that we can cluster according to similarities of attitudes toward products, product usage, or needs. To be effective in marketing, we must be able to collect our potential and current customers into clusters that represent similarities of needs. In this way we can deal with any number of segments and offer each segment our new products with benefits that will match their needs.

Market Segmentation

Segmentation refers to the process of dividing our potential markets for new products and services into distinct subgroups of current or potential customers so we can reach them with a distinct benefit mix, making our marketing efforts more effective. The advantages of market segmentation become more profound when used with the new needs analysis presented in Chapter 4. As Leon Schiffman states:

> The marketer who is able to subdivide his market into distinct segments of consumers *with different needs* [emphasis added] and interests is in the position to develop marketing mixes that specifically appeal to the needs of each segment. Prospects are more likely to identify with messages specifically tailored to their needs. Because it is carefully targeted at a specific group of consumers, a market segmentation strategy is sometimes called the "rifle" approach to marketing. On the other hand, an undifferentiated marketing strategy, which tries to be all things to all people, is usually referred to as a "shotgun" approach, because it scatters its appeal to a mass audience made up of diverse types of people. As such, it usually ends up meaning very little to anybody. (Schiffman and Kanuk 1978, p. 14)

Over the last few years marketers have employed a number of different approaches or characteristics for segmenting their current or potential markets. These criteria might include a demographic segmentation, geographic or socio-cultural segmentation.

Based on our findings, as presented in Chapter 4, we believe the psychographic segmentation becomes the most effective clustering for new product development. We must fulfill our customers' needs, and our psychographic model has been shown to be quite effective in providing direction for that task.

There are, however, several other types of segmentation which we can use for special situations. These are not recommended for initial new product segmentation as they can be misleading in terms of identifying the underlying needs of prospective customers. Once these underlying needs have been properly identified, then other types of segmentation might be useful. These would include:

- Demographic
- Geographic
- Buying behavior
- Family life cycle
- Race and nationality
- Religion
- Social class
- Psychographic

Keep in mind that the customers within each of these segments will have different needs, so it is misleading for us to assume that just because some may be in the same social class that they will have the same needs.

They may share similar needs, but their specific needs will be quite different. Let's look at these potential segments in a little more detail to see how they support our needs theory.

Demographic Segmentation

Demographic characteristics such as age, gender, education, and income are the most commonly used for market segmentation. These are, perhaps, the most easily measured statistics of a potential population or target group. Also, once measured and segmented, the groups can be associated with product usage. This, however, gives us no clue as to what these various segments desire, or need, in products or services that have not yet been developed to satisfy those unfulfilled needs.

We liken this type of research to a photographic snapshot. It can give you a clear understanding of the conditions that exist at a given moment, but cannot provide us with an indication of what is needed but not yet fulfilled. Our new communication theory provides the insight to what is needed.

There are many different methods of segmenting markets demographically. Some of the more popular ones are described in the following sections.

Age

Age is a demographic variable that is closely linked to product usage. Teenagers have very different needs for products and services than do adults, or the retired or "gray" market. All of these groups can be associated with specific needs or product desires.

Many markets are closely linked to the shifts in age groups, and the new product market must be constantly aware of, and monitoring, the subtle and not-so-subtle shifts in age groups. For example, consider the new product opportunities of the following known shifts, as reported by the Census Bureau:

- In 1955 there were 25 births per 1,000 population in the United States. Today there are only 15.7 births per 1,000 population. Think about the new product implications of that, as we will have relatively fewer younger people and an aging population over the next few years.

- By year 2000, households in the 35–49 age group will account for 35 percent of the population. In 1985, that group accounted for only 25 percent of the population.

This is one reason why Kellogg's has been emphasizing "adult" cereals, even putting $55 million behind ProGrain and Nutri-Grain.

Exhibit 5.1 dramatically illustrates the shift toward a gray market by the year 2000.

Another factor to consider is that *teenagers* will have a discretionary budget of nearly $75 billion by the year 2000, up from $50 billion in 1986.

Gender

Yes, there are still differences between males and females. In this age of unisex everything, from hair styles to clothing, from cosmetics to jewelry, we tend to blend the sexes in the name of equality. However, in the marketing world we still contend with significant differences between the sexes.

Even today there remain lively debates among marketers over the relative importance of men and women, particularly in the purchase of consumable products. Most marketers agree that the woman is still the most important, having significant influence over both the *purchase* decision and the *brand* decision. This varies by product category, of course, but the female wields significant clout in purchase decisions.

We must remember that our needs and our attitudes vary greatly. Nowhere is this more significant than in the gender segment. As Schiffman states:

> Sex has always been a distinct segmentation variable, though in recent years it has become less clear in discriminating product usage. However, women are still the prime users of such products as hair coloring and cosmetics, and men of cigars and shaving preparations. (Schiffman and Kanuk 1978, p. 15)

When planning new product development, we must consider some significant factors, such as the following:

1. The position of women as controllers of income and wealth; they may not earn it all, but they control most of it

2. Women have extreme influence as purchasers for the family; consider, for example:

   - More than 40 percent of all individual wealth is owned by women

   - Life insurance companies pay women over $750 million a year

   - Sixty percent of all estates go to women, only 25 percent to men

The increasing significance of women as marketing targets for new products is reflected in the growth trends shown in Exhibit 5.2, which reports the relative balance of men and women in the work force.

Exhibit 5.1

U.S. Civilian Labor Force and Participation Rates: 1970–2005 (Projected)

Race, Sex, and Age	Civilian Labor Force (millions)						Participation Rate (percent)					
	1970	1980	1990	1994¹	2000 proj.	2005 proj.	1970	1980	1990	1994¹	2000 proj.	2005 proj.
Total²	82.8	106.9	124.8	131.0	141.8	150.5	60.4	63.8	66.4	66.6	68.2	68.8
White	73.6	93.6	107.2	111.1	118.8	124.8	60.2	64.1	66.8	67.1	68.7	69.3
Male	46.0	54.5	59.3	60.7	63.8	66.0	80.0	78.2	76.9	75.9	76.0	75.3
Female	27.5	39.1	47.9	50.3	55.1	58.8	42.6	51.2	57.5	58.9	61.8	63.6
Black³	9.2	10.9	13.5	14.5	16.0	17.4	61.8	61.0	63.3	63.4	65.5	66.2
Male	5.2	5.6	6.7	7.1	7.8	8.3	76.5	70.3	70.1	69.1	70.8	70.5
Female	4.0	5.3	6.8	7.4	8.2	9.0	49.5	53.1	57.8	58.7	61.2	62.6
Hispanic⁴	(NA)	6.1	9.6	12.0	14.3	16.6	(NA)	64.0	67.0	66.1	68.0	68.4
Male	(NA)	3.8	5.8	7.2	8.7	9.6	(NA)	81.4	81.2	79.2	80.2	79.5
Female	(NA)	2.3	3.8	4.8	5.8	7.0	(NA)	47.4	53.0	52.9	55.8	57.3
Male	51.2	61.5	68.2	70.8	75.3	78.7	79.7	77.4	76.1	75.1	75.3	74.7
16 to 19 years	4.0	5.0	3.9	3.9	4.4	4.6	56.1	60.5	55.7	54.1	55.4	55.5
20 to 24 years	5.7	8.6	7.3	7.5	7.2	8.1	83.3	85.9	84.3	83.1	84.0	84.4
25 to 34 years	11.3	17.0	19.8	18.9	17.2	16.5	96.4	95.2	94.2	92.6	93.1	93.5
35 to 44 years	10.5	11.8	17.3	19.0	20.7	19.6	96.9	95.5	94.4	92.8	93.7	93.5
45 to 54 years	10.4	9.9	11.2	13.0	15.8	18.1	94.3	91.2	90.7	89.1	90.4	90.2
55 to 64 years	7.1	7.2	6.8	6.4	7.7	9.6	83.0	72.1	67.7	65.5	69.1	69.7
65 years and over	2.2	1.9	2.0	2.2	2.1	2.2	26.8	19.0	16.4	16.8	15.0	14.7
Female	31.5	45.5	56.6	60.2	66.6	71.8	43.3	51.5	57.5	58.8	61.6	63.2
16 to 19 years	3.2	4.4	3.5	3.6	4.2	4.2	44.0	52.9	51.8	51.3	52.0	52.4
20 to 24 years	4.9	7.3	6.6	6.6	6.4	7.2	57.7	68.9	71.6	71.0	72.5	73.6
25 to 34 years	5.7	12.3	16.0	15.5	14.9	14.8	45.0	65.5	73.6	74.0	78.1	80.7
35 to 44 years	6.0	8.6	14.6	16.3	18.8	18.6	51.1	65.5	76.5	77.1	83.0	86.2
45 to 54 years	6.5	7.0	9.3	11.4	14.7	17.4	54.4	59.9	71.2	74.6	79.7	82.8
55 to 64 years	4.2	4.7	5.1	5.3	6.2	7.8	43.0	41.3	45.3	48.9	50.3	52.4
65 years and over	1.1	1.2	1.5	1.7	1.6	1.7	9.7	8.1	8.7	9.2	8.5	8.8

NA Not available. ¹See footnote 2, table 626. ²Beginning 1980, includes other races not shown separately. ³For 1970, Black and other. ⁴Persons of Hispanic origin may be of any race.
Source: U.S. Bureau of Labor Statistics Bulletin 2307; *Employment and Earnings,* monthly, January issues; *Monthly Labor Review,* November 1993; and unpublished data.

Exhibit 5.2

Relative Changes in the Number of Men and Women in the Labor Force

Index Numbers

Year	Males	Females
1970	100	100
1975	110	119
1980	120	144
1985	126	162
1990	131	176
1995	135	190

Source: U.S. Bureau of the Census, *Statistical Abstract of the United States, 1995* (Washington, D.C.: U.S. Government Printing Office, 1995), p. 372.

Income

Income, of course, is always an important consideration in segmenting our potential customers. In business-to-business marketing it is less of a consideration because, in most cases, the customer's corporation or business will be paying for the new product.

However, as we market products in a business-to-business environment, we must realize that real people in your customer organization will be evaluating the product or service, and they will be conducting that evaluation based not only on their company's needs, but also on a W.I.I.F.M. perspective. What will this new product do for them—will it help them achieve new goals and status within the organization, will it help them create a better environment for customer service?

We cannot overlook the important considerations of understanding not only corporate needs, but also personal needs within the marketing mix. Consider, for example, the personal needs of many women as they enter the work force, and how these can have a significant influence on our new product development program:

- One in four working women has a child of 12 years or under
- One-fifth of these have children under 2 years of age
- Working women with children under 1 year of age increased from 31.6 percent of workers in 1977, to 51.9 percent in 1987, only a ten-year span (U.S. Dept. of Labor 1994, p. 399)

Do these statistics give us some opportunities for new products and services? Let's understand working women's needs and create some new products for them.

Education

Education has always been, and is becoming increasingly important as a segmentation variable. Customers who achieve high educational levels often have different product and service needs, and usually have a higher discretionary income to fulfill those needs.

These people are far more discriminating in what they desire and buy, and, as marketers, we must approach them very differently. In business-to-business marketing most of our customers will be better educated than in the mass markets, putting a particular burden on us to have a complete understanding of their needs.

Education is always interrelated with age, income, and occupation. We must always keep in mind that the customer with a better education may:

- Be less affected regarding *what* they buy than *how* they buy, and how they are influenced by promotion and advertising
- Be more discerning, more discriminating, more rational buyers
- Be less responsive to persuasion

To understand the impact of education regarding the ability to purchase goods and services, consider the relationship between education and income shown in Exhibit 5.3.

Occupation

Occupation is always a significant factor in determining the needs of our potential customers. Customers' needs vary greatly based on the roles they play to generate income for their families or organizations. Consider for example the different desires or needs of the following groups:

College students versus the retired couple—The college student's desire for the latest CD or video game differs from the retired couple's desire for an ocean cruise or a new set of golf clubs.

Blue collar versus white collar—The white collar worker, lodged in Maslow's esteem category and wanting a new Mercedes, is meeting different needs than the blue collar worker who desires a pickup truck so he can haul materials on the weekend.

Professional versus nonprofessional—The nonprofessional administrative worker has different needs than the physician or lawyer that he or she may consult with on a regular basis.

Artist versus engineer—A right-brain oriented artist, a conceptual thinker, has different thought processes and needs than the left-brain oriented, lineal-thinking engineer.

Exhibit 5.3

Influence of Education on Income

Education Level	Median Income (1995)
Elementary School	
Less than 8 years	$13,920
8 years	17,965
High School	
4 years	28,700
College	
1–3 years	35,220
4 years or more	56,118

Source: U.S. Bureau of the Census, *Statistical Abstract of the United States, 1995* (Washington, D.C.: U.S. Government Printing Office, 1995), p. 470.

We are all different, with totally different needs. As we pursue jobs and careers, we adopt the needs associated with success in those tasks, and these needs vary by occupation function, and by individual within those functions.

Geography

Our customers' needs are materially affected by differences in climate, topography, and the general character of the section of the country in which they reside. The needs of people living in Boston or New York are significantly different from those living in Laguna Beach or Tucson. Some of these differences include the following:

Social customs—The black-tie dinner party in Marblehead or Newport, RI, will involve very different customs from the week-end hoedown with the cloggers in Asheville, NC. Likewise a barbecue in the Southwest becomes a clambake or a cookout in the Northeast. These are very different settings, very different customs, and very different needs are associated with each of them.

Dress—Would your customers in New York City consider wearing their bikinis on the boat for a cocktail party and cruise in February? Would your customers in Tucson be likely to wear a fleece-lined Chesterfield coat to the country club in March or

April? Probably not, but if you reverse the geography, the dress would be more appropriate. Where are your customers, and what are their needs?

Types of recreation—The author spent several winters on the East Coast officiating, through a race committee, the activities of frost-bite sailors. These skippers of small dinghies would congregate every Sunday morning at the yacht club, from December through March, to race the little eight-foot sail boats. These races involved dodging ice packs, temperatures of below zero, and death within four minutes if they capsized and weren't plucked from the icy water. In California, during these same months, recreationists are riding their mountain bikes and jogging on the beach. Their needs vary accordingly.

Types of homes—Having remodeled an 1899 Dutch Colonial home in Greenwich, CT, then, years later, building a mountain retreat in Bailey, CO, the author can assure you the needs are very different! The needs for heating and lighting systems are similar, but Malibu lighting just doesn't go well in Greenwich. And propane heating is not in the vocabulary in lower Fairfield County, CT. In Bailey, the deep well and rural electricity seem to work just fine. But in Greenwich these are foreign concepts. Our needs are very different, even based on the types of homes we buy. Think of the apartment dweller, for example, whose needs are vastly different from those of the self-contained mountain person living in the seclusion of the Colorado Rockies.

Types of Foods

Having lived in the South, on the West Coast, the East Coast, and, now, in the Rocky Mountains of Colorado, the author has experienced a wide variety of culinary delights. Our friends in Boston have a knack for making scrumptious baked beans, but they don't know anything about black-eyed peas and collard greens. Our friends in southern California are into fajitas, flautas, and fennel, but they've never shared the delights of fresh elk or antelope right off the grill, as the lone eagles of Bailey enjoy.

Food preferences vary greatly because of geographic dispersion. As we try to communicate with customers in various parts of our country, we must realize that our feeling about the great clam chowder we created last night just doesn't relate to the person who just created a great jambalaya last night. And the fried okra can't relate to the oyster stew. Our needs are different.

Take a look at Exhibit 5.4. Note the differences in seafood consumption between the Northeast and the Midwest. These differences translate into needs that vary by geography.

Exhibit 5.4

Some Regional Differences in Food Purchases (average weekly expenditures in dollars)

Item	All Consumer Units	Northeast	Midwest	South	West
Cereals and cereal products	1.50	1.64	1.47	1.40	1.52
Beef	4.10	4.56	4.03	3.94	3.89
Poultry	1.50	1.80	1.25	1.54	1.44
Fish and seafood	1.14	1.42	0.86	1.06	1.29
Eggs	0.66	0.70	0.57	0.68	0.70
Dairy products	4.79	5.31	4.72	4.24	5.09
Fruits and vegetables	5.86	6.52	5.37	5.39	6.38
Sugar and other sweets	1.26	1.26	1.29	1.15	1.39

Source: *Consumer Expenditures, in 1993,* U.S. Bureau of Labor Statistics tables, pp. 718–722.

Buying Behavior

For many products there is a heavy skew, or bias, toward the heavy users. When developing new products for these categories we must be aware of these potential biases, and use them to our advantage.

In many product and service categories 80 percent of the purchases are made by fewer than one-third of the potential population. Only one-third of the population currently smokes cigarettes, for example, but it is a billion-dollar plus industry. Other examples of buying behaviors that affect product usage follow:

- Isn't it amazing that over 80 percent of the car rentals are made by less than 5 percent of the population?

- How many times do we purchase a particular brand because it has been the family tradition to do so for so many years? If it is good enough for mom, it is good enough for me!

- Or we purchase a specific brand because our neighbor, significant other, or close friend uses it and swears by its effectiveness.

So buying behavior is influenced by many factors. As new product developers, we must be accepting of these "givens" and try to understand the needs that are driving this behavior.

Family Life Cycle

As families grow together they pass through a pattern of predictable consumption habits. All of these are important stages of development, but they have very different implications as to attitudes and needs. Consider the different needs of the following three families:

- Family A, head of household is age 42, they have two children
- Family B, head of household is age 38, they also have two children, not living with them, but with other parents
- Family C, head of household is age 42, they have no children

Assuming they all have relatively the same income and education, and all live in the same geographic region, isn't it clear they all have different needs to fulfill? Each family has its own separate needs, and they will gear their purchase patterns accordingly.

Importantly, they all fall into the same demographic category, but look at how different they are in terms of lifestyle. This is why we must break the opinion barrier and learn about their attitudes toward life.

Race and Nationality

The United States is quite unique in many ways, but our "melting pot" composition truly separates us from most other nations. We are populated by many different races and nationalities.

New York City, for example, is populated, roughly, by 25 percent Anglos, 25 percent Jewish, 25 percent blacks, and 25 percent mixed of Hispanic, Asians, and "all others." In Los Angeles, the majority race is now Hispanic, but Hispanics only account for about 8 percent of the population nationally. Washington, D.C. and Detroit are heavily influenced by the black culture, yet blacks only account for 12 percent of the national population.

These race and nationality differences have tremendous impact on our quest to identify needs among intended target audiences. Whether they be consumers of our customers' products, or buyers and planners of new product development in our customers' offices, these cultural influences must be understood.

These race and geographic considerations become very important in new product development. Consider the population skews shown in Exhibit 5.5 as you plan your new product development program.

Religion

People's religious orientation maintains a strong grip on their attitudes and resulting behavioral patterns, particularly for some more orthodox

Exhibit 5.5

The Top Ten Black and Hispanic Cities

Metropolitan Area	Black Population (thousands)	Percent of Population
New York	2,102.5	28.7
Chicago	1,087.7	39.1
Washington, D.C.	922.8	26.0
Detroit	777.9	75.7
Philadelphia	631.9	39.9
Los Angeles–Long Beach	546.5	14.0
Houston	458.0	28.1
Baltimore	435.8	59.2
New Orleans	307.7	61.9
Atlanta	264.2	67.1

Metropolitan Area	Hispanic Population (thousands)	Percent of Population
New York	1,783.5	24.4
Los Angeles–Long Beach	1,492.8	38.1
Chicago	545.8	19.6
San Antonio	520.3	55.6
Houston	450.5	27.6
Riverside–San Bernardino	426.0	21.3
El Paso	355.7	69.1
Anaheim–Santa Ana	275.1	49.1
Miami	267.2	59.2
San Diego	229.5	20.7

Source: *1994 County and City Data Book,* U.S. Department of Commerce, Bureau of the Census.

religions. For years Catholics only ate fish on Fridays, and Jews never ate pork. Religious beliefs are so strong among some sects that they affect many areas of the adherents' lives, resulting attitudes, and consequent behavior patterns, including the following:

Clothing. The Hasidic Jews, the Amish, the Hare Krishnas and others all have distinct attitudes regarding clothing. Calvin Klein probably won't be able to sell these members new products for some time in the future.

Recreation. Members of the Church of Christ, or of the Latter Day Saints, don't flock to nightclubs, or even to private parties where there is dancing or alcohol consumption. Don't try to change their attitudes if you're introducing a new line of fine wines or liqueurs.

Marriage Relationships. Many orthodox religions impose severe restrictions on marital partners. Jehovah's Witnesses, for example, are not allowed to marry outside of "the order" or they will be banned for life.

Personal Habits. Other covering laws, or enforced attitudes, of religious groups include restrictions on smoking, consumption of alcoholic beverages, even consumption of beef. These restrictions have a major effect on how our customers perceive our potential new products, and we must be aware of these biases.

Social Class

A person's goals, attitudes, value system, standard of taste, and the resulting behavioral patterns are largely influenced by the social world in which they grew up and in which they currently live. In spite of what we may wish, the person who grew up in a wealthy family in Newport, RI, is quite different from the same demographically identified person who grew up in a ghetto in East Los Angeles.

People's social class has considerable influence on their attitudes and behavior patterns. According to Maslow, people seek to fulfill a need for belongingness, for being with persons of similar interests and capabilities. This has a tendency to keep us lodged in a social class that is comfortable for each of us.

Social classes are determined by such factors as family background, education, occupation, the neighborhood in which people live, and the sources and amount of income. Compounding the complexities of sorting out the impact of social class on new product development, is that there is a considerable psychological and social distance between the three top social classes and the mass of people immediately below them, as shown in Exhibit 5.6.

Psychographic Segmentation

Psychographic segmentation refers to the intrinsic characteristics of individuals. These would include their lifestyle, interests, attitudes, and even

Exhibit 5.6

Characteristics of Social Classes

Class	Approximate Percentage of the Population	Characteristics
Upper upper	5	The "aristocracy" of a community, the old-line families with inherited wealth who can live comfortably on income derived from investments.
Lower upper		Families with newly gained economic and social power.
Upper middle	20	Families in which head(s) of household are likely to be successful business executives or professionals. Their incomes average somewhat less than the people in the upper classes and derive predominately from salary and current savings rather than from invested wealth.
Lower middle	65	White-collar workers, tradespeople, a few skilled workers, and their families. They have accumulated little property but are frequently homeowners.
Upper lower		Skilled and semiskilled workers who participate relatively little in educational and other advantages of our society.
Lower lower	10	Unskilled laborers, people on relief, unassimilated foreign groups. Many of them are poor and lack the ambition and/or opportunity to improve their lot.

personality type, any personal characteristic that would influence their attitudes toward products and services. As Schiffman states (p. 16):

> Psychographic research is designed to identify consumer differences on a wide range of psychological and social-cultural characteristics. To more fully understand what psychographic characteristics are, it is useful to contrast them with demographic characteristics.

This is a very important consideration, because individuals with an identical demographic identification may have vast differences in buying behavior based on their psychographic makeup. For example, a 25-year-old single female, a recent college graduate, earning $40,000 a year, living in San Francisco, may be living the "good" life, attending lots of parties, a free spirit, a high-spending romantic. Another single female with the same demographics may be quite frugal, watching every dime she earns, carefully doling out every penny of her $40,000 paycheck, tucking most of it away for that "rainy day."

The same demographics, but very different lifestyles and behavior patterns. Our projective research technique would indicate two totally different people, different attitudes, and different motivations and resulting buying behaviors. A demographic profile of potential buyers can be very misleading. We advocate a psychographic segmentation first for new product development, to be supplemented later, perhaps, with demographic segmentation for media and other marketing considerations.

Values and Lifestyles Segmentation

One of the most widely used models for segmenting a population based on psychographic considerations is VALS, an acronym for Values and Lifestyles System. VALS was developed by Stanford Research Institute (SRI) some years ago, and recently has been updated with VALS II. The original VALS identified six segments of the population, based on psychographic considerations:

1. *Outgoing optimists* are outgoing, innovative, community-oriented, positive toward grooming, not bothered by delicate health or digestive problems or especially concerned about germs or cleanliness.

2. *Conscientious vigilantes* are conscientious, rigid, meticulous, germ fighting, with a high cleanliness orientation and sensible attitudes about food. They have a high cooking pride, a careful shopping orientation, and tend not to be convenience oriented.

3. *Apathetic indifferents* are not outgoing, are uninvolved with family, are irritable, have a negative grooming orientation, and are lazy—especially in terms of cooking pride.

4. *Self-indulgents* are relaxed, permissive, unconcerned with health problems, interested in convenience items but with relatively high cooking pride, and self-indulgent toward themselves and their families.

5. *Contented cows* are relaxed, not worried, relatively unconcerned about germs and cleanliness, not innovative or outgoing, strongly economy oriented, and not self-indulgent.

6. *Worriers* are irritable, concerned about health, germs, and cleanliness, negative about grooming and breakfast, but self-indulgent with a low economy and high convenience orientation.

The second VALS analysis added a segmentation that implied some personality types were outer directed, inner directed, or need driven. This model is shown in Exhibit 5.7.

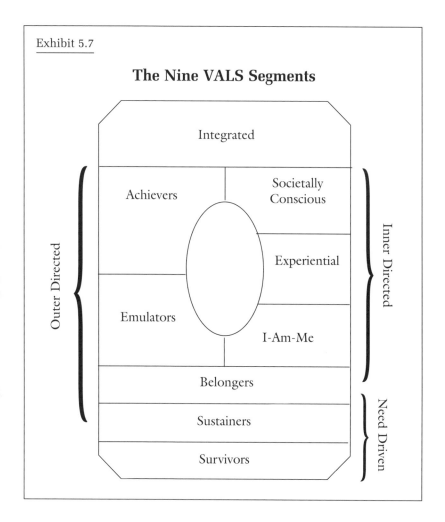

Exhibit 5.7

The Nine VALS Segments

Integrated

Achievers

Societally Conscious

Experiential

Emulators

I-Am-Me

Belongers

Sustainers

Survivors

Outer Directed

Inner Directed

Need Driven

Factors to Consider in Directing Products to Specific Market Segments

In addition to the specific demographic and psychographic considerations above, there are other product-related features which we can control. These features can be converted to benefits by understanding our customers' needs These would include the following:

Packaging: Are we clearly communicating the character of the brand? Are we creating an appeal to our customer, or to the end-user? Have we conducted tests to be certain we have the right graphic and functional mix?

Quality: We often misinterpret attitudes toward quality, measuring instead our customers' opinions, which might reflect the consensus of the reference group. We cannot incorporate all of the potential or desired qualities into one product. We must select the most meaningful according to our selected target segments. We can have several different segments, with different qualities, as explained in Chapter 6.

Price: Price is usually related to size and quality, but must be carefully researched to determine how well the benefits satisfy the needs. Customers are willing to pay for need satisfaction. Price is often a dominant factor, and the size and quality may have to be altered accordingly, to bring congruence with need satisfaction. For many products price is a significant indicator of quality.

Unit of sale: We must determine the best size of the package, the size most closely fulfilling the customers' needs. Anheuser-Busch, for example, learned that there are a lot of heavy Budweiser drinkers out there, and that a 12-pack was more convenient than the traditional 6-pack. Do you need a 6- or a 12-pack? Is a *family* of products more advantageous for you than a single item? Cosmetics and HBA marketers have learned that family packs work best for them.

Brand image: All of the above relate to how consumers perceive the product—which brings us back to perceptions, the mental picture people carry of a product or service. Ideally, we must strive for a unique image, as we discuss in Chapter 6. Consider the unique images created for: Marlboro, Virginia Slims, Volkswagen (the original "Bug"), and BMW.

Product concept testing: Projective testing is critical at this stage, to be certain your product is satisfying important needs. If it is not, modify it or forget it. Consumers must be able to perceive the product in terms of the satisfaction it delivers.

Product positioning: Perceptual positioning fits a product into an existing scheme of things in our customers' minds. You can fill a gap among existing brands by manipulating the features of the product. Try to be different from the competition by learning what they represent to customers, then positioning yourself as being different from them. Positioning is an important concept, and we explore it in more detail in Chapter 6.

CHAPTER
6

Linking Benefits to Needs— Making the Sale

One of the common misconceptions about the role of advertising is that it creates a demand for products and services. While advertising is an important part of the marketing mix, advertising alone cannot create demands for products—it cannot coerce customers to buy something they don't want.

For advertising, or any other marketing element, to create a buying situation, there must already exist a predisposition, a need, for the product or service. Advertising is powerful, but a need or desire must exist, either consciously or unconsciously, before our promotional efforts can become effective in causing action.

If we have completed the proper research and have identified unfulfilled needs, then advertising can stimulate the desire and motivate buying behavior. Advertising alone cannot create needs, only help our customers become aware that the need exists, and that there is a desire for need fulfillment.

In new product development our task is to convert our product features into benefits, then *link those benefits to the needs* we've discovered through research. That linkage is how we position our product in the minds of the customers. There are several theories on how to best accomplish this linkage, depending on the type of product or service we are introducing. These will be described below.

But first, think about sports cars for a moment. Who makes the finest sports car available today? Who makes the second best? What about computers? Who makes the best computer? The second best? Or airlines. Who is the best airline flying today? The second best?

In each of these categories, and others as well, we usually have a good idea of who we think is the best, the second best, and so on. The brand or service that achieves the top spot in your own brain has achieved that *position* through a combination of advertising, promotional, and word-of-mouth messages. You have a perception that they are the best, a perception formulated by many different perceptions and experiences you have had with it or the competition.

Most marketers and advertisers try to influence our perceptions with their messages, but the position we assign in our brain is controlled by us. We assign that position because of our basic needs, and how we believe the product will help us fulfill those needs.

Positioning recognizes the inherent differences in people, and that we all have different needs, at different times. Since it is impossible for all people to want to buy the same brand or service, we must select those target audiences for which ours has the best appeal, that satisfies the more important needs. New product development is really a battle for a piece of the customer's brain. We must give our product a meaning that distinguishes it from our competition.

Positioning—Getting inside the Heads of Our Customers

In their seminal book *Positioning: The Battle for Your Mind,* Al Ries and Jack Trout presented a new strategy that suggested that effective product marketing involved creating a position or a niche in the minds of your customers in a way that differentiates your product from all others.

> Positioning starts with a product. A piece of merchandise, a service, a company, an institution, or even a person. Perhaps yourself.
>
> But positioning is not what you do to a product. Positioning is what you do to the mind of the prospect. That is, you position the product in the mind of the prospect.
>
> So it's incorrect to call the concept "product positioning." As if you were doing something to the product itself.
>
> Not that positioning doesn't involve change. It does. But changes made in the name, the price, and the package are really not changes in the product at all.
>
> They're basically cosmetic changes done for the purpose of securing a worthwhile position in the prospect's mind.

Positioning is also the first body of thought that comes to grips with the problems of getting heard in our overcommunicated society. (Reis and Trout 1981, p. 2)

Once a position has been established, all subsequent advertising and promotional materials should support it, to stabilize it in the mind of the customer. This should be so well entrenched that the customer will always consider your product or service every time a similar need arises. An effective position promises need gratification with each mention of the product.

The concept of positioning is particularly important in a competitive market. In these cases you want your product or service to be *perceived* differently, more distinctly from competition. This is similar in scope to Rosser Reeves's *unique selling proposition* (USP), discussed below.

Be First, and Be Right

The Trout and Reis agency also proposes two additional considerations to support their positioning theory. They believe your product's advertising message must be *first* and it must be *right*. Being first means you should be the first in your category to make a claim, and being right means being on target with your customers' needs, being on strategy.

The importance of being first allows a preemptive claim. It doesn't matter that others in your category may be able to make the same claim. If they haven't said it and you do, you're first. You are in the power position. Jack Trout illustrates the importance of being first by asking:

Who was the first man to walk on the moon? Who was second?

Who was the first man to fly solo across the Atlantic? Who was second?

Who was the first person you ever kissed? Who was second?

His point is that more than likely we can recall who was first, but we have difficulty remembering who was second or third. Some advertising illustrations are provided later in the chapter, but do you recall which automobile campaign was first to ask us to "Think Small"? Or the first "Uncola" out of the many that could have said it?

Being right, or relevant, means you must understand your customers' needs and guide your product's benefits to fulfill those needs. You must be on strategy, meaning that your uniqueness, your theme, your advertising, must connect with the target audience.

Volkswagen did their homework and knew there was a sizable portion of the automobile market that was tired of big gas-guzzling cars, chrome, and tail fins. They urged these potential customers to think small, and they did. Relevant. 7-Up learned there was a large market that was tired of, or just didn't like cola drinks. So they were the first Uncola. Relevant. Marlboro was the first macho male cigarette, and Virginia Slims the first female cigarette. Also relevant.

Developing a uniqueness and presenting it first, and being relevant to the needs of your customers, must work together. You can have one without the other, but it will result in weak positioning, and a sure formula for new product failure.

Reinforcement

Being first and being right isn't even enough if you don't reinforce your message with repetition. We've learned that repetition is greatly needed in the learning process, and it's no different in new product work, or establishing new claims.

Ideally, we recommend repetitive messages over a long period of time, rather than grouping them in shorter periods. This is highly contingent upon strategic and budget considerations, of course, but consistency is important.

Consistency leads to campaigns. A campaign must hammer home a singular message, consistently, over a period of time. VW stuck to the "Think Small" campaign for years, whereas David Ogilvy's brilliant work for Rolls Royce did not result in a campaign. Bill Bernbach's highly memorable ads for Levy's Jewish Rye only received limited poster and newspaper exposure, but his brilliant campaign for Avis ran for years. Consistency.

Changing Needs Offer Positioning Opportunities

With Maslow, and inherent in our own Perception Expansion Theory presented in Chapter 4, is the concept that no need is ever fully satisfied, and that new needs keep emerging with personal and cultural changes. Since needs keep changing, they present motivational opportunities for fulfillment. This results in marketing opportunities for a constant flow of new products and new positionings.

Most luxury car buyers probably don't know specific safety records of automobiles in that category. But it doesn't matter—Mercedes has pre-empted the safety claim. They were the first, and it is certainly relevant. However, a friend's analysis of why he bought a Mercedes illustrates the usefulness of our Perception Expansion Theory in identifying customers' ever-changing needs:

Wayne is an upper socioeconomic southern California advertising executive who recently bought a new Mercedes. He justified his decision based on his needs:

Wayne, how did you justify your decision to your wife?

I just told her how safe she and the kids would be on those rainy nights.

Wayne, what about your accountant?

Oh that was easy, I just explained that the Mercedes has a very high resale value, and that it was an investment, not an expense.

Your friends?

Oh, I just assured them how great they'd feel riding in a new Mercedes instead of my current car.

Wayne, why did you *really* buy the Mercedes?

Because of my personal power needs, the need to look good in my environment. I feel great in that car!

So while people may justify our actions based on opinions—other people's opinions—they are ultimately motivated by their individual needs. We can be certain that the preemptive safety claim for Mercedes is reassuring a lot of mothers out there, and this helps ease the sale for the Waynes of the world who want it for other reasons.

There are a lot of products and services being offered, each vying for a piece of the potential customer's mind. You've got to find an acceptable manner to elbow your way to the front to get the attention of your customer. Proper positioning is a sure way to accomplish this, and it relies heavily on understanding your customers' needs, and how they distill incoming data and process it into their needs hierarchy.

Develop a Creative Strategy

Most good copywriters work from a creative platform that assesses the basic elements to be considered in developing a positioning for a product. These would include the primary benefits of the product, the target audience, competition, and other relevant considerations. This strategy combines these considerations and helps lead to the development of a unique position in the minds of the customers.

Developing a creative strategy helps us focus on the really important elements, those that will respond to the customers' needs. It also isolates the target market(s) and shows us how to motivate their behavior. There are many different types and styles of creative strategies, but one simplistic and effective strategy can be outlined as follows:

Creative strategy:

To convince _____

To buy _____

Instead of _____

Because _____

This creative strategy, when completed by the creative team, may look something like this:

Convince—Males, 25–44 years old

To buy—BMW

Instead of—Mercedes

Because:

- It's more exciting to drive
- Better styling makes me look better
- More youthful appearance
- More "with it" contemporary feeling

Mercedes, of course, would develop their own creative strategy that presents their primary benefits, linking them to their target audiences. This type of strategy can be used with any type of product or service. It works as well with package goods as it does with business-to-business products. A typical business-to-business application might be:

Convince—Purchasing agents at Fortune 500 companies

To buy—(Upgrade to) Windows 95 software

Instead of—Current software

Because:

- More user friendly
- Easier to learn
- Greater employee productivity
- Greater savings on new purchases

Linking Benefits to Needs

Now that we've established that all customers have needs that are unfulfilled, and always evolving, and that we can create products and services with benefits that match those needs, how do we make the link? There are many theories offering advice on how to do that, but there are two main ones that have been refined and widely practiced over the years.

Unique Selling Proposition (USP)

In the early 1960s Rosser Reeves, at Ted Bates Advertising, developed a strategy of finding a unique selling proposition with every product or service. He even proposed that if a product just didn't have one, if it was a truly parity product, it was advisable to make one up—which the agency did regularly.

According to Reeves, the USP must be preemptive, or *new*, as Trout and Reis would say today. This means that no other product or service in your category can say this, as you have preempted the positioning as your own. Reeves believed that every product advertised should possess *or imply* superior benefits that would result in greater awareness and memorability of the brand. Some examples, old and new, of the USP include the following:

USP	Brand
Think small (Exhibit 6.1)	Volkswagen
The ultimate driving machine	BMW
Does she . . . or doesn't she? (Exhibit 6.2)	Clairol
We're only #2, we have to try harder (Exhibit 6.3)	Avis
Drive it like you hate it (Exhibit 6.4)	Volvo

Brand Image

David Ogilvy, founder of Ogilvy & Mather agency, proposed the *brand image* strategy in the late 1950s. He sought to lift potentially parity products above the competition by giving them a very positive image, preempting the leadership role from the competition. He said, "Give your product a first-class ticket through life." Some of his successes are shown in Exhibits 6.5 through 6.8.

Exhibit 6.1

Volkswagen Ad

Think small.

Our little car isn't so much of a novelty any more.

A couple of dozen college kids don't try to squeeze inside it.

The guy at the gas station doesn't ask where the gas goes.

Nobody even stares at our shape.

In fact, some people who drive our little flivver don't even think 32 miles to the gallon is going any great guns.

Or using five pints of oil instead of five quarts.

Or never needing anti-freeze.

Or racking up 40,000 miles on a set of tires.

That's because once you get used to some of our economies, you don't even think about them any more.

Except when you squeeze into a small parking spot. Or renew your small insurance. Or pay a small repair bill. Or trade in your old VW for a new one.

Think it over.

Exhibit 6.2

Does She . . . or Doesn't She? Ad

Does she...or doesn't She?

Hair color so natural only her hairdresser knows for sure!™

On a clear crisp day, in brightest sunlight, or in the soft glow of a candle, she always looks radiant, wonderfully natural. Her hair sparkles with life. The color young and fresh, as though she's found the secret of making time stand still. And in a way she has. It's Miss Clairol, the most beautiful, the most effective way to cover gray and to liven or brighten fading hair color.

Keeps hair in wonderful condition— soft, lively—because Miss Clairol carries the color deep into the hair shaft to shine outward, just the way natural hair color does. That's why hairdressers everywhere recommend Miss Clairol and more women use it than all other haircolorings. So quick and easy. Try it **MISS CLAIROL** yourself. Today. *HAIR COLOR BATH is a trademark of Clairol Inc. ©Clairol Inc. 1962*

Even close up, Miss Clairol looks natural. The hair shiny, bouncy, the gray completely covered with the younger, brighter, lasting color no other kind of hair-coloring can promise—and live up to!

Exhibit 6.3

Avis Ad

When you're only No. 2, you try harder. Or else.

Little fish have to keep moving all of the time. The big ones never stop picking on them.

Avis knows all about the problems of little fish.

We're only No. 2 in rent a cars. We'd be swallowed up if we didn't try harder.

Avis can't afford to relax.

There's no rest for us.

We're always emptying ashtrays. Making sure gas tanks are full before we rent our cars. Seeing that the batteries are full of life. Checking our windshield wipers.

And the cars we rent out can't be anything less than spanking new Plymouths.

And since we're not the big fish, you won't feel like a sardine when you come to our counter.

We're not jammed with customers.

© AVIS RENT A CAR SYSTEM, INC.

Exhibit 6.4

Volvo Ad

Drive it like you hate it.

When Volvo came to the U.S. from Sweden in 1956, Chevy was the "hot one," Ford was the "safe one" and Volkswagen was just catching on as the "funny one."

We'd like to say that Volvo immediately caught on as the "tough one." It didn't.

At first only the "car nuts" bought it. They figured that if a Volvo could hold up under Swedish driving (no speed limits), survive Swedish roads (80% unpaved), withstand Swedish winters (30° below), that a Volvo would hold up under anything.

They figured right. Volvos were driven tight off showroom floors onto race tracks where they proceeded to win more races than any other compact ever made.

Volvos are still winning races. But that isn't why they're bought today. Volvos are now being used and misused as family cars. They're safe. And on the highway they run away from other popular-priced compacts in every speed range, yet get over 25 miles to the gallon like the little economy cars.

Volvo is now called the "tough one." And it's the biggest-selling imported compact in America today.

You can drive a Volvo like you hate it for as little as $2565.* Cheaper than psychiatry.

*Manufacturer's suggested retail price East Coast Port of Entry. Overseas delivery available. See the Yellow Pages for the Volvo dealer nearest you.

Exhibit 6.5

Schweppes Ad

The Man from Schweppes Arrives!

Mᴇᴇᴛ Commander Edward Whitehead, Schweppesman Extraordinary from London, England, where the house of Schweppes has been famous since 1794.

The Commander recently arrived in these United States.

His mission? To make sure that every drop of Schweppes bottled in America has the *original flavor* which has made it the essential mixer for Tonic drinks all over the world.

Schweppes flavor, you will notice, is curiously refreshing. Schweppes has an almost astringent impact on the palate, with a delicious *bittersweet* aftertaste.

Today, the original Schweppes elixir (that's what gives Schweppes its unique

flavor) is being imported from England and bottled in America. And now that Schweppes have given up the extravagant practice of transporting heavy bottles across 3,000 miles of Atlantic Ocean, you can buy their incomparable Tonic, for little more than ordinary mixers, at stores everywhere.

It took Schweppes almost a hundred years to bring their Tonic to its present perfection. But it will take you only thirty seconds to pick up the phone and order Schweppes from your storekeeper.

* * *

RETAILERS: For prompt service, please call Pepsi-Cola Bottling Co. of Pittsfield, 158 Tyler St., Pittsfield, Mass. Dial: 4579.

Schweppes
Qᴜɪɴɪɴᴇ Wᴀᴛᴇʀ

Schweppes now available in handy 6-bottle cartons of 10-oz. bottles.

Exhibit 6.6

Hathaway Ad

Note the square-cornered cuffs on Baron Wrangell's shirt—a celebrated Hathaway hallmark.

Hathaway presents <u>Antique Ivory</u>—a color that never clashes

EVER noticed the marvelous color that ivory goes when it ages? It lies somewhere between cream and old gold. Very unobtrusive. Very soft. A perfect color for a shirt.

When Hathaway's experts were finally satisfied that an *Antique Ivory* dye could be made, we chose to present it on our famous all-cotton Batiste Oxford. You see the result above. A mellow color that refuses to clash with anything.

Hathaway pioneered Batiste Oxford many heat-waves ago. This remarkable stuff retains the look and handle of top-grade Oxford but sheds nearly half the weight. It never feels sleazy the way some summer shirtings do.

The shirt above costs about $7.50—long or short sleeves. See the full range of Hathaway Batiste Oxfords at the better stores. They're also in White and Bermuda Blue. For store names, write C. F. Hathaway, Waterville, Maine. Call OXford 7-5566 in New York.

Shirts in Antique Ivory stripes, about $7.50; solids, about $7.

Exhibit 6.7

Rolls Royce Ad

"At 60 miles an hour the loudest noise in this new Rolls-Royce comes from the electric clock"

What <u>makes</u> Rolls-Royce the best car in the world? "There is really no magic about it—it is merely patient attention to detail," says an eminent Rolls-Royce engineer.

Exhibit 6.8

Jamaica Ad

Spend a glorious day at the Newcastle Army Training Camp on Blue Mountain. Don't laugh. You'll have one hell of a good time.

Newcastle is one of the few army posts in the world with no AWOL problem. In fact, it's so ruddy beautiful up there, 3850 feet up Blue Mountain, with the hummingbirds dipping all around, and the Bougainvillea and honeysuckle winding over the veddy British/Colonial/Victorian buildings, and the cool, tickly hillcountry air, and the puffy clouds sailing by *under* the windows, and the 40-mile view of Kingston and the sea, and the deep gorges filled with birdsong—that the army sometimes has trouble getting the troops to leave when their training cycle's over.

We have the same problem with the civilians who visit here.

Just so you don't forget, amid all this tropical scenic splendor, that you're still on an Army post, the "management" has kindly laid out a series of mountain marches for you. (All voluntary, of course.)

Start your training easy—with a short 20-minute hike up a gentle curving path—called reassuringly, The *Ladies'* Mile. If you get your wind, you can build up to the almost vertical Catherine's Peak trip. ("Mountain goats, 25 min.; Gentlemen, 40 min.; Ladies, 55 min.; Old Soldiers and Young Children, 1 hr. 5 min.")

If Shank's Mare is not your

speed, you can always rent a mule (although be forewarned: walking is faster). The mules and their masters work out of a town called Mavis Bank. To the top of the mountain and back, it's $8.40 for mon and beast. (The mon goes along to keep the beast honest.) Make an overnight trip out of it with a stay at Whitfield Hall, a rough-it hostel near the peak. $1.40 per night. It's not as plush as army life. But after all, one must make *some* sacrifices these days.

For more vacation (or enlistment) information, see your travel agent or Jamaica Tourist Board, Dept. 8N, 630 Fifth Ave., New York City 10020.

CHAPTER
7

Building Value-Added Concepts for New Products

Your customers *want to buy your new product or service,* because it helps them satisfy their needs. Yet in over 90 percent of new product introductions, marketers inappropriately communicate their product's benefits, thereby not satisfying those needs. We give our customers reasons to *not* buy our products.

It's a paradox that customers want to buy our products and services to satisfy their needs and feel better about themselves, but we don't give them a support system to motivate their behavior. We haven't learned what their true needs are, nor have we found an effective way to answer their question of "What's in it for me?"

This brings us to the concept of value-added product positioning. Value-added positioning helps our customers find ways to perceive added value, additional benefits, to the new product concept, even beyond the intrinsic benefits we have provided them. This helps them justify or rationalize a purchase decision by providing some additional benefit that may not actually be part of the physical characteristics of our product or service. That is the essence of our Perception Expansion Theory (P.E.T.).

Just as our friend Wayne, in the last chapter, found several ways to justify his purchase of a new Mercedes, the real reason he bought it was that it made him feel great, playing to his need for esteem and power. The *added value* was that his wife would feel safer driving with the kids, he had made a good investment, and his friends would feel good arriving at the club in a Mercedes. These are not actually part of the physical or mechanical attributes of the car, but they are there for Wayne to enjoy. He expanded his perception of what the Mercedes actually is—he became proof of our P.E.T.!

There have been many great, brilliant positioning strategists that could build value-added new product concepts. One of the best we've worked with is Mary Wells, founder of the highly successful agency Wells Rich Greene, Inc. Mary has had many successes over the years, including Braniff Airlines (R.I.P., but not her fault!), Benson & Hedges 100's, Love Cosmetics, Bristol-Myers, Wesson Oil, to name but a few. Mary has a unique capability of seizing an opportunity to create value-added concepts. She says of her abilities, "I have . . . a greater talent for putting information together and coming up with a way to sell a product than I have for actually putting the words together." This was uttered after a successful stint as a copywriter with a Detroit department store and a very successful New York advertising agency prior to her founding of Wells Rich Greene, Inc. Positioning and value-added concept development is a talent that is critically important in new product development.

Adding Perceived Value to Products

By adding perceptual value to products and services, we can more effectively fulfill our customers' needs, making the new product more valuable to them. This is the essence of new product positioning strategy—to find and expand that perceptual value that will turn a prospect into a customer. A brilliant execution of a weak strategy won't make a product successful—that's why so many new products fail. But even a weak execution of a brilliant strategy will more often succeed with a new product introduction. The perceptual positioning is the entire ball game. Give your customers a reason for expanding their perceptions of your product.

Finding that most effective way to sell a product, service, idea, or institution is the key to success. A strategy must never lose sight of its purpose. It must go beyond facts and call upon that creative insight that each of us possesses—we must not be confused by facts, rather we must try very hard to determine what our customers want, in spite of the facts.

Once insight takes over, the facts will blend into the subconscious to become an integral part of the creative process. Once we let insight and facts mentally percolate we achieve creative breakthrough. As Maslow said, that's the "Ah Hah!" moment.

Questions to Ask in Positioning Your Product

John O'Toole, another master of positioning products, has said:

> Strategy is information that bright, creative, analytical minds have synthesized into a sort of blueprint for making ads . . . it is developed from the answers to these questions:
>
> 1. Who or what is the competition?
> 2. Whom are we talking to?
> 3. What do we want the prospect to know, feel, or understand?

In creating new products or services, how do these questions really apply? Who or what is the competition?

- Similar brands.
- Not always similar brands—when MasterCard was introduced there were no other credit cards. The competition was the stigma attached to using credit.
- When Sunkist decided to try to expand their market the competition was not orange juice, rather snacks of various types.

Whom are we talking to?

- Demographics versus psychographics—what is the role of lifestyle in the purchasing decision, what are the attitudes toward the product or category?
- Campbell Soup successfully marketed Soup For One to a market with changing eating patterns.
- Talk to them directly—advertising works best as a dialogue between two human beings.

What do we want the prospect to know or feel or understand?

- Who is the audience, what are their attitudes?
- What is our point of difference (unique selling proposition)?
- Identify the desire, the want, problem, dream, then relate that to a benefit of the product or service.

The McCann-Erickson agency uses a role-playing model within their creative department to try to develop answers to similar questions. One of their training sessions uses a hypothetical product called Just Curls. Just Curls is a gel which, when washed into the hair, temporarily curls it. The curl lasts until it is washed out with regular shampoo. In their role-playing session the following questions are asked:

1. Whom are we talking to?
   - Females, 21–35 years of age.
   - They probably envy the more daring hairstyles of their friends.
   - Their hair is more or less straight, uninteresting.
   - They perceive themselves as being on the "drab" side of style and grooming.

2. Where are we in the mind of this consumer?
   - Do I need to spend big money on a perm, and then hope that it works?
   - Whom shall I trust?
   - I'm really sensitive about my hair.
   - I'll just hack it all off and forget about it.

3. Where is our competition in the mind of this consumer?
   - I can't afford to throw away money on a bad perm.
   - Scares me just to think about it—me in a perm?
   - I even rolled my hair once—took forever—and I'll never do it again.
   - I just don't have time for such things.

4. Where would we like to be in the mind of this consumer? (Positioning)
   - Imagine that, Just Curls really does something.
   - I massage it in after the shampoo.
   - Suddenly my hair is curly, and I just let it dry.
   - Can't wait for Saturday night.

5. What is the consumer promise? (U.S.P.)
   - Just Curls does what my hair needs.
   - I don't have to think twice about using it.
   - I can be someone other than my drab self—someone fun!

6. What is the supporting evidence?
   - It's easy to use
   - Just massage it into wet hair, then let the hair dry naturally.
   - I'm having more fun because of my "new" hair.
   - I feel better about the way I look.
   - My life seems better, I'm feeling better about myself.

7. What is the tone of voice for the advertising?
   - Empathetic.
   - Provides hope for someone who's tried everything.
   - Feeling good about yourself makes you feel like a different person.
   - Hair is not the end-all of one's life, but it communicates much about us to others.
   - It's important to have your hair looking the best it can.

Meeting Basic Human Needs

Another agency, Doyle Dane Bernbach, Inc., has developed a list of ten basic human needs. Their advertising for existing and new products must fit within at least one of these needs. The needs, and the types of products that are prevalent with the need, are as follows:

1. To be popular, attractive, and feel wanted (health and beauty aids, cosmetics, fitness programs)
2. To have material things (fads, luxury items)
3. To enjoy life through comfort and convenience (luxury items, home furnishings, microwaves, VCRs)
4. To create a happy family situation (travel, entertainment, looking good to them)
5. To have love and sex (health and beauty aids, cosmetics, fashion)
6. To have power (designer labels, sports cars, private clubs, esteem)
7. To avoid fear (security systems, smoke alarms, insurance)
8. To emulate those you desire (snob appeal, stylish items)
9. To have new experiences (travel, innovative products)
10. To protect and maintain health (healthy foods, exercise products, health clubs)

Some Successful Strategies

Still others have developed the following strategies for new products that work for them, some of which we've already explored (products representing each strategy are listed as well):

1. *The generic strategy:* There is no competition, and thus no need for a claim of superiority. Arm & Hammer baking soda, for example, uses a generic strategy.

2. *Preemptive claim:* Uses a claim that has not yet been exploited, even though there is little to distinguish the product from the competition. An example is the ketchup race—Heinz always lost because it was thicker.

3. *The unique selling proposition:* Promotes a lasting competitive advantage consisting of a unique physical characteristic or benefit. Examples include Crest toothpaste and BMW.

4. *Brand image strategy:* Psychologically based, not physically based. The emphasis is on emotions, not facts. Examples include Mercedes, Rolls Royce, and AT&T.

5. *Positioning strategy:* Emphasizes how we want to be positioned in the mind of the customer—how this brand is different and superior. Avis, Volkswagen, and IBM are examples.

6. *Resonance approach:* Focuses on situations or emotions that evoke positive associations, such as nostalgia. Kodak and Hallmark use a resonance approach.

7. *Affective strategy:* Seeks to make contact on a purely emotional level, and to break through indifference to evoke change of the customer's perception of the product. Chanel No. 5 (Share the Fantasy), Calvin Klein, and Guess Jeans use an affective strategy.

The Perception Grid

Another approach to positioning new products links the customers' perceptions of importance of the concept, how much they think of it and how much they feel about it. This utilizes a questionnaire and a grid, shown in Exhibit 7.1, that measures and quantifies their perceptions on four levels, then plots their attitudes about new concepts.

Depending upon the quadrant your customer falls into, you can conclude how he or she may react to a new product concept. The quadrants and their respective attributes and products are as follows:

1. *Thinking/high importance:* In the thinking/high importance quadrant, the customer is a thinker who places a high importance on purchasing this product. The customer needs a lot of information about the product. The product is important to the customer, and he or she will raise logical questions about it. Typical products in this quadrant will be cars, homes, appliances.

2. *Feeling/high importance:* In the feeling/high importance quadrant, the customer relies less on data or hard information and

Exhibit 7.1

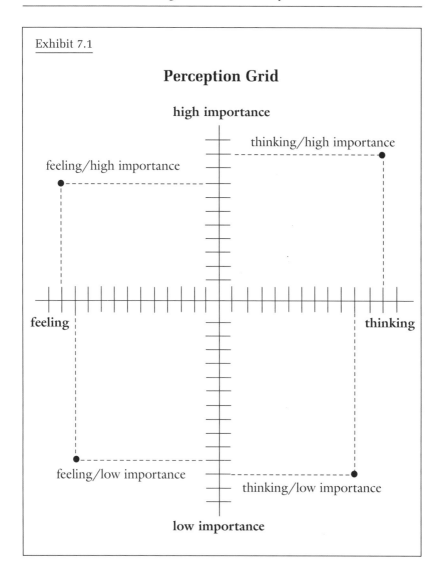

Perception Grid

high importance

thinking/high importance

feeling/high importance

feeling

thinking

feeling/low importance

thinking/low importance

low importance

relies more on attitude. Products are usually related to self-esteem, such as jewelry, cosmetics, and fashion apparel.

3. *Thinking/low importance:* In the thinking/low importance quadrant, customers usually indulge in habit formation. The customer is a doer, and product decisions are made with minimal thought. Reminder messages are sufficient to induce purchase. Products in this quadrant are mostly household, cleaning, food, and personal care items.

4. *Feeling/low importance:* In the feeling/low importance quadrant, the customer is a reactor, buying products that satisfy personal

tastes. Customers have a peer group orientation or impact. Advertising messages should be designed to gain attention. Products in this quadrant include cigarettes, beer, liquor, and snacks.

Tips for Creating a Successful Strategy

Another theory for building value-added positioning for new products is in creating four ingredients for a successful strategy: simplicity, specificity, durability, and advertisability.

Simplicity—make it understandable, and the old adage, K.I.S.S.—Keep it simple, stupid. Don't expect your customers to be able to comprehend too much at one time. They have other things on their minds, and they don't want to be distracted by you.

Specificity—get to the heart of the problem quickly and relate the product to their needs. Be as specific as possible regarding your benefits that will help satisfy their needs.

Durability—develop a strategy that will have staying power, that will last for years if it is continually refreshed. As one agency said, your campaign should have legs, so it can run for a long time, delivering the same unique selling proposition in new and exciting ways.

Advertisability—the basic campaign idea, the strategy, must lend itself to a number of different executions, each with an important message. The strategy should work executed in television, print, point-of-sale, or direct mail.

Other strategic development considerations to get to the big idea in new product introductions should include five features built into your initial promotional materials:

1. They must be written with specific audiences in mind.

2. They must distill large amounts of information into limited space or time.

3. They must bristle with vitality.

4. They must possess substance—what's the unique selling proposition, the big idea.

5. They must be presented with reader ease in mind—short words, short paragraphs, simple sentences. Get to the idea in a hurry.

Very important in preparing promotional materials for your new product or service is the presentation of the big idea—how do we express it in the headline or main statement of our leading promotional piece. David Ogilvy said it quite succinctly: "Headlines are five times more likely to be read than the related text." Typically, headlines deal with gratification or needs (human interest or other aspects of affect), or utility (news, benefits, or rewards). But they deal with our customers' *needs,* on one level or another.

Headlines help us break through the clutter we face every day. *Communication clutter* exists for every individual in the new information society. Estimates are that every city dweller in the United States is exposed to about 3,400 commercial messages a day. Therefore, consumers engage in selective exposure, relying on availability, potential utility, congruence with existing attitudes, and need gratification to select messages and to reduce the communication clutter to a manageable level.

Gestalt Theory of Communication

The Gestalt theory of communication suggests that phenomena that are perceived as similar tend to be assimilated or grouped and integrated, or placed in the same mental file, providing a simpler information structure. Thus, new product introduction campaigns that group messages from various media, and effective headlines that relate the main communication objectives regardless of the media used become critical to unifying the message for our customers.

Breaking through the Clutter

As we write or supervise the writing of the introductory advertising copy for our new products, we should strive to break through the clutter. We do this by saying something that will grab the attention of our intended customers, a U.S.P. presented in an exciting, attention-getting manner. Some of the accepted ways of accomplishing this in advertising copywriting are:

1. Stick to the present tense if possible.
2. When possible, use singular nouns and verbs.
3. Use active verbs, which mean action.
4. Stick to familiar words and phrases.
5. Vary the length of sentences and paragraphs.
6. Write conversationally, even to the point of using contractions.
7. Punctuate properly, even in headlines.
8. Refrain from bragging, remember W.I.I.F.M.
9. Avoid superlatives, vague words, and clichés.
10. Support improbable, unbelievable facts with evidence.

11. Involve the reader.

12. Don't set out to make an advertisement.

13. Revise, revise, revise.

14. Tell the reader enough, but just enough.

15. Make the strange familiar and the familiar strange.

16. When you have a revolutionary idea to promote, it may be more effective to play it straight.

17. Use understatement.

CHAPTER
8

Ideation

When we start with the premise that all of our customers have needs, and that they want to have those needs fulfilled, it is not a quantum leap to understand that they will help tell us how to fulfill them. It's in their best interests. If we give them the proper stimulation, our customers will help us build winning concepts to satisfy their needs. The essence of the Perception Expansion Theory is that our customers will expand their perceptions of a concept until it satisfies their needs. We can then modify the concepts to match their expanded perceptions.

The key to the theory is to give them the right stimulation, and that's where development and use of concept boards becomes critical. We must provide an environment in which customers can comfortably relate to us those needs that are not being fulfilled, and the benefits they believe will fulfill them. This requires some stimulation from us, and the concept boards provide that. But we should not assume that the concepts we develop will be perfect coming off the drawing board.

It is important to understand that the P.E.T. process *begins* with the concept boards, and evolves from there. We keep modifying the concepts based on new, expanded information obtained from the interviewing process. The final concepts usually bear little resemblance to the beginning boards, particularly in the copy, as we continually rewrite to make them more appropriate to the needs we discover. We literally build them to meet the needs.

The graphic format we use for the boards is 11" × 14", small enough to be used in one-on-one interviews, but large enough for all participants to see in focus group settings. The boards are drawn by hand with color marker pens so as to replicate as closely as possible the environment of the product usage, which McGuire found to be very important. We write the copy on the reverse side of the boards so it can be changed easily, and the interviewer can make notes for future versions.

We discipline ourselves to go through several steps while developing the concept boards, steps that are very important to getting to the proper starting point. While the initial idea generation is only a starting point, it is important to cover all possible features and benefits in order to properly stimulate need identification.

Start with a Clean Slate

We often have trouble convincing clients to set aside their personal and organizational biases, and to "take off the blinders," so to speak, so every potential and appropriate new product can be explored. It is very important to begin the idea generation process with a clean slate, so that these other environmental concerns will not dictate the direction of the process.

Our potential customers have needs to be fulfilled, and those needs are seldom, if ever, related to the personal, organizational, or technical constraints of our organization or favorite product categories. We can't allow ourselves to start a new product development project with the biases inherent in an organizational system, as that would put too many limitations on the development process and could restrict finding the winning combinations.

Begin with the attitude that anything is possible. First identify the need, the opportunity, then find a way to produce a solution later. If you can't produce the idea with current technology, perhaps someone else can, and you can license the idea to them. It is very difficult for some executives to get beyond the "currently available technology" syndrome. They become mired by today's knowledge, or their own organization's capabilities, overlooking that someone, somewhere, may be developing a new technology that will solve the problem and result in a successful new product.

If a new product concept is strong, and there is a sizable potential market for it, this will have an effect of leading technology development. Where technology is needed, and it is possible and profitable, it will be developed. Just remember the line in a movie of a few years ago, "Build it and they will come."

Input Sessions

Our first step in the idea generation process we call *immersion,* or *input sessions.* We gather all of the people involved in the new product development project and have them provide all of the relevant information already generated.

The group usually consists of marketing people, market research, R&D, project leaders, advertising, anyone whose input could be relevant to the project. During these sessions we probe for any ideas that anyone may have already come up with, any thoughts that have been tucked away in filing cabinets, any relevant research regarding the market or the product, anything that could possibly be of value to the project. This is the analysis stage, to analyze exactly where we are, to gather as much information as possible.

During the input session it is important to get everyone's expectations out on the table. When you leave the session there should be a very clear understanding of the objectives of the project. These objectives should be very specific, dealing with timing, revenues, and other relevant considerations. Examples of specific objectives might be to:

- Create a minimum of three successful new products or services for the food service industry that are compatible with our current channels of distribution, or that could be marketed through new channels of distribution without substantial increase in cost

- Create new products that will generate at least $25 million each in incremental revenues to the organization

- Develop the products for test marketing, or regional marketing, during the fiscal year

By setting very specific goals the new product development team has a clear understanding of what's expected from the project. A management benefit is that revenue forecasts can be anticipated, and the development team becomes accountable for meeting or surpassing the goals.

Incubation

The second part of the Perception Expansion Theory ideation phase, *incubation,* requires an enforced period of time in which we allow ourselves a calm, almost detached, even dormant process during which we absorb all of the factual data that has been generated during the input session. These factual data are assimilated and at the conscious level, and we need to let the data be absorbed into the subconscious level.

It is at the subconscious level that the intuitive process takes over, and helps us start solving problems, or gaining insight. As Freud speculated, it is this intuitive process of the preconscious or inductive level of the mind that interprets the factual data and allows us to begin analyzing it in a problem-solving manner.

This is a period of dormancy during which we generate a solution or solutions to the problem. These ideas, or solutions, are being created without our use of deductive thinking. As part of the creative process we seem to need to be able to remove ourselves from the logical or deductive part of the process for a while, and let the intuitive forces of the preconscious part of our brain take over. There is mounting evidence that we must enforce periods of removal from the factual or logical, and allow innovation and creativity to take over at the subconscious level, seemingly unencumbered by logic and facts.

Illumination

As mentioned above, Maslow referred to the next phase, *illumination,* as the "Ah Hah!" stage. This part of the creative process occurs as our brain is finishing the incubation stage and is ready to start serving up some ideas or insights for us to develop. This normally follows incubation and allows our insight, creativity, and imagination to coalesce with the factual data we assimilated at the conscious level.

This is where we can say "Now I get it!" and start generating ideas that are pertinent to the problems we are trying to solve. We all seem to have this capability, but we don't all utilize it to its fullest extent. Many of us have trouble slipping into the incubation stage—we are driven by organizational constraints or personal pressures to get the problem solved quickly. It is important, however, to indulge in the incubation process to get to the "Ah Hah!" stage and gain insight on the problems.

Allen Hurlburt, in his book *The Design Concept,* illustrates it this way:

> Anatomy of the mind: This diagram illustrates Sigmund Freud's three major levels of consciousness. The top is the conscious level, the receptor of information, and at the bottom is the unconscious. In between, Freud locates the preconscious, the level that draws on both of the other levels and provides the source for insights and inspirations. The left side of the diagram illustrates the intellectual processes, and the right side, the emotional (see Exhibit 8.1) response. The circled numbers indicate the four generally accepted steps in the creative process: (1) Analysis, or Input, (2) Incubation, (3) Inspiration (Illumination), (4) Verification.

Note that Hurlburt uses different terms to apply Freud's theories to the creative process.

Idea Generation

Idea generation can take many forms. The most common of these is probably the brainstorming session, which involves getting a group of

Exhibit 8.1

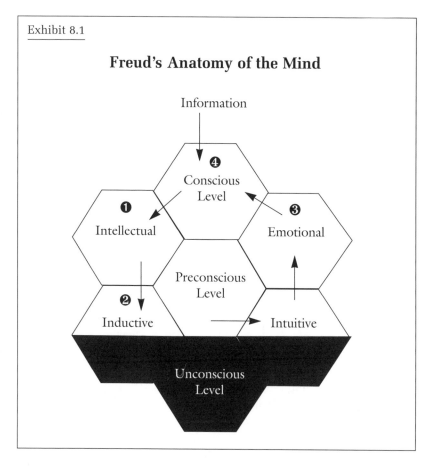

Freud's Anatomy of the Mind

people together to focus on the "Ah Hahs" that have emerged from the illumination stage. By getting together to share thoughts and illuminations, the idea is to use the session to spark new ideas and breakthroughs.

To be successful, a moderator should focus on one topic or subject at a time. Members of the group will then share their ideas that have come to them as a result of the incubation period. The moderator will encourage others to jump in with theirs and to "leap-frog," take the solutions to new areas that might be beneficial to the customers in satisfying their needs. By using this free-association method group members create new ideas and new insights.

Another popular idea generation method is a group dynamic called Synectics, developed by Synectics Inc., in Cambridge, Massachusetts. The Synectics approach requires some role playing by a would-be customer who presents some problems to the small group of participants. The group quizzes the "client" on his or her problems and offers solutions to fulfill the needs.

A moderator records the solutions on large boards or flip charts for later editing. While this is similar to brainstorming, it is more directed toward the customer, and the process can last for several days, with participants adding new ideas as they become immersed in the process and the incubation period takes over.

There's No Such Thing as a Bad Idea

No matter which idea generation session you select for your group, it is very important to encourage a quantity of ideas, and not to be judgmental about any of them. Even though an idea submitted may seem weak at first, it could spring other, perhaps stronger ideas later on. It is important to explain this to the group in advance.

During the session it is more productive to simply record the ideas with a pledge to go back later for more thorough evaluation. There is no such thing as a bad idea, because any idea can lead thinking into new areas of consideration. Encourage participants to let fly with any and all thoughts.

We recommend beginning each idea generation session with a stimulus of known ideas and a discussion of any unfulfilled needs of the customer base. The Perception Expansion Theory was followed exactly as outlined for the case study presented in Chapter 13. The project began with an input session, as described above. The project was a new product exploratory for the home office worker and telecommuter, to determine problem areas and unfulfilled needs. The client was the Public Service Company of Colorado (PSCo).

During the input session data had been presented that outlined the general segments of the market, and group members submitted ideas for some potential concepts and brand names. Discussion guidelines were prepared that covered these areas, and urged participants not to be prematurely judgmental. These guidelines were used to establish a positive environment for a productive session. The actual guidelines used are shown in Exhibit 8.2.

Go for Quantity, You'll Hit Quality

As the session proceeds encourage the participants to strive for as many new ideas as possible, without regard to whether they are good or bad, manageable or not. If you strive for quantity, good ideas will happen as part of the process, or by combining several weaker ideas into one strong one.

From the idea generation session, over 100 ideas were generated in little over an hour. There were some very strong concepts, some weak ones, and some that fell clearly in the middle. But from those we were able to combine and strengthen some, and ultimately culled 28 new ideas that we elected to develop and put through the P.E.T. process. These are shown in Chapter 13.

Exhibit 8.2

Sample Discussion Guidelines

I. Idea Generation Guidelines

- **Purpose**—To generate a broad range of product, service, and marketing concept alternatives that might appeal to the various customer groups. New product ideas, new services, new market positionings, and any potentially relevant concept will be encouraged. The purpose is to expand our thinking as broadly as possible, to remove mental parameters from existing marketing conditions.

- **Explore the needs of the**

  —Home worker

  —Corporate managers

  —Government

- **No limits**

- **No retribution**

- **No such thing as a bad idea—critiquing comes later**

II. Segments

- *Full-Time Self-Employed*—Own their own business and work at home more than 30 hours per week

- *Telecommuters*—Work at home for an employer eight or more hours a week during typical office hours.

- *Spillover*—Bring work home from their full-time job at least 16 hours (2 days) per month after regular work hours.

- *Moonlighter*—Have one full-time job and earn extra income outside of that job by working at home for another employer.

- *Part-time self-employed*—Work in the home less than 30 hours per week at their own business and have no other income.

- *Entertainers*—Spend time at home on-line or playing computer games for entertainment purposes.

Continued

III. Issues/Needs
General
- Isolation
- Distractions (fewer?)
- Stress reduction
- Idea generation/distribution
- Voluntary/Involuntary home placement

Corporate
- Increased productivity
- Reduced pollution
- Reduction of office space
- Need for a measurement system

IV. Potential Concepts
- Surge protector
- Energy back-up system
- Wall size monitor
- Auxiliary energy lines
- Ambient lighting system
- Comfort providers
- Energy packages (consultation)
  - —Computer package
  - —"Gallery"
  - —Safety
  - —Security
  - —Weatherproof (won't go down)
  - —Conference room/area
- Remote FAX retrieval
- Insurance issues
- Appliance service contracts

V. Potential Names
HomeWork Solutions
Home Station
Home Base
Lone Eagle Network/Nest
Virtual Office

Become the Customer

Another way to lead an idea generation session is to put yourself in the environment of your customers. Become a customer for a while and think about their needs.

- What do you perceive as their problems?

- What are they doing now to solve them?

- What can you do to help them solve them easier, faster, or more economically?

- Have they said things to you that indicate there may be unfulfilled needs?

- What do you think they would like you to do for them?

- How could you provide them better service?

- What have they told you recently about your product or service, either positive or negative?

Explore Potential Benefits

A segment of the idea generation session should also focus on benefits. This would include current benefits of your product or service, *potential* benefits of your product or service, or the benefits that may be desired by your customers and potential customers.

Often we indulge complacency as we become absorbed in the organizational routine, and we don't take the time or make the effort to continually examine our existing product base. Sometimes there is a new product concept already sitting there, just waiting for some modification of an existing product.

Don't Be Limited by Current Technology

We cannot overstress the importance of not being limited to current technology. Idea generation sessions are used to help solve problems and identify opportunities. We cannot be constrained by whether a new idea can be developed immediately. With the plethora of corporate right-sizing in recent years, there are many good, creative out-sourcing capabilities available.

Very often, if an idea is strong enough, some of these sources will work with you on a royalty basis, saving up-front development costs. But the more important consideration is that it is not uncommon for innovation to lead production. Thomas Edison had a need for illumination, developed an idea for a light bulb, *then* found a way to produce it.

Granted, it doesn't always happen that way, but it often does, and we should not let this limit our creativity.

Just the Beginning

In order for the P.E.T. concept to be most effective, we must stress that the idea generation stage is just the beginning of the process. We are not trying to come up with the answers at this time, we are only trying to come up with effective graphic stimuli so that in a research situation our customers can respond in an insightful and creative manner. This will then help us to identify, then help us solve their problems.

Too often the idea generation process ends at this stage. When a project director walks out of a brainstorming session with 25 new concepts, he or she is often deluded into thinking that somewhere in the batch must be at least three winning concepts. This is the critical fault of most new product programs.

At this stage the 20 or 25 concepts are handed over to the market research department, which will then conduct mall intercept interviews, central location tests, or focus groups, and have the respondents vote on which of the group of concepts they prefer, or rank them in order of priority. The concepts are not used to probe for additional needs that are *not* being met, rather we are asking our potential customers to tell us which of these potential new product concepts they prefer. They may not want any of them, as none of them satisfy their needs, but we don't ask them that.

The P.E.T. process requires that we not ask our customers (respondents selected from their target markets) to vote on the concepts they like most, rather we use the concepts as probe stimuli to determine how we can modify the concepts to have them satisfy their needs. This is a major change in research techniques, and is critical to developing more successful new products and services.

Concept Board Development

A lot of care and creativity must go into the development of a concept board. We are using the boards to generate reaction from our customers (respondents) during interviewing situations, not as advertisements, as some copywriters and art directors are trained to create.

The objective of the board is to present one major benefit, simply stated. The headline and copy should be crisp, clear, easy to understand, and come to the point, the benefit, very quickly. As you'll see from the ads shown in the previous two chapters, the benefit is quickly and simply stated so the respondent knows immediately *what's in it for me*.

The graphic, or illustration, used should also be benefit related and support the main idea in the headline. Recall McGuire's findings that concepts are communicated more effectively if they are presented in an environment that is familiar. So keep the graphics simple and friendly so your respondents don't have to dig for the main benefit.

Some of the concepts used in the PSCo project, described in Chapter 13, were a little more complex out of necessity. A few of the ideas had multiple benefits and we wanted the respondents to grasp them quickly so we illustrated the major ones together on one board.

Again, the environment created by the board is very important. Try to use real people and situations that are nonthreatening to the communication process. We are digging for information with the boards, not trying to sell products. So leave the clever, witty advertising presentations for another time.

Exploration and Expansion

The *exploration* stage is the most critical to the success of the Perception Expansion Theory, as this is where it becomes abundantly clear that P.E.T. is very different from other approaches. It is during this stage that the original concept boards that have been created are evolved into winning concepts with the help of our customers.

It is important that our customers be fairly represented in the interviewing process. Each interviewing group of respondents should be balanced to be reflective of the demographics or psychographics of the target markets. And remember, due to the expansive nature of the interviewing process, new target markets may emerge. This is particularly true in business-to-business research, where respondents are typically in the business arena and are aware of unfulfilled needs in areas outside their own.

Focus Groups

Focus group interviews are often used to validate direction on new product development, or to obtain confirmation that the basic concept, already developed internally, will be acceptable in the marketplace. Focus group sessions usually consist of 5 to 10 respondents who are representative of current users or potential users of a product or service.

This type of directed brainstorming usually focuses on what *is*, rather than focusing on what *is not*, or what is needed. As covered in Chapter 2, the P.E.T. strategy is to *un*focus the group to determine what they are not being provided. Focus groups of this type are useful for consumer products or services, where there are no competitive concerns among the respondents.

In-Depth Personal Interviews

For the business-to-business marketer the in-depth, one-on-one interview is usually preferable, as it can be conducted within assurances of confidentiality, with no threat of competitive espionage.

In personal interviews, once the interviewer has developed sufficient rapport with the respondent, the respondent is more likely to be open about his or her feelings, thus permitting us to probe and break the opinion barrier. Also, the respondents are not intimidated by other respondents in the room and feel more comfortable sharing ideas and talking about their needs.

Explore Every Influencer in the Channels of Distribution

With the P.E.T. process, every individual in the channels of distribution that has contact with a new product or service has a potential impact on the ultimate sale. Therefore, it is important to obtain their input on the new product concept before major development funds are committed. They often have greater influence than we realize on the promotion and marketing of the new product or service, and their early input can be critical to the ultimate success or failure of the program.

First, they will feel better about positively marketing the new product when it's launched, because they will feel they've had a role in the development of it. If they've been asked about their suggestions and been a part of the research process they will have a more positive outlook later.

Second, each member of the channel of distribution gets you a step closer to the end-user, where the final buying decision is made. The clerks in retail outlets hear more comments about products than we do. The regional sales manager for our synthetic fiber example certainly gets more customer feedback than the corporate marketing executives, so it's important to include them in the loop.

To help identify all of the potential influencers in your channels of distribution, the following checklist can be used as an initial guideline for planning. This list is not complete, of course, because every industry is different, with different monikers for the function. But here's a starting point:

Marketers:
- Manufacturer
- Converter
- Licensee
- Packager

Sales:
- Broker
- Agent
- Representative
- Direct

Wholesalers:
- Distributor
- Jobber
- Broker
- Wholesaler

Retailers:
- Mass merchandisers
- Chains
- Independents
- Franchisees
- Direct
- Pyramid

Consumers:
- Retailers
- Shopping networks
- Pyramid
- Catalog
- Direct response

The P.E.T. Interview

The proper projective type interview is very important to the P.E.T. process, whether it be through a focus group or individual in-depth one-on-one format. One-on-one interviews are semistructured and can tell us a lot about individual customer reactions to potential new products and services. The individual interview is preferable in business-to-business research, as discussed above.

The individual interview is also preferred in many consumer projects due to sensitive subject matters, or when the group process does not allow enough time to probe for deeper issues. So the individual in-depth interview has definite advantages in some situations.

It is with some degree of pride we have based the P.E.T. on Hermann Rorschach's inkblot tests, and Dr. Ernest Dichter's motivation studies, and have contemporized their theories through our recent studies. Both used projective techniques to try to delve beyond the conscious mind to uncover more deeply held motivations.

The P.E.T. strategy uses contemporary concept boards instead of inkblots, as the respondents can feel more comfortable in a familiar environment. However, the end result is the same. P.E.T. breaks the opinion barrier (the conscious stated opinions) and delves into the more subconscious, the attitudinal level that is usually cloaked by the conscious-level opinions.

There are some distinguishing characteristics between the P.E.T. in-depth interview and other techniques used:

- There is a heavy emphasis on "why" questions.

- There is a heavy emphasis on probing, e.g., "Can you tell me more about that?"

- The concept boards are used as projective techniques.

- Respondents are encouraged to tell us what is wrong with a concept, how it can be improved, to *project* their own needs into the situation.

- Respondents are challenged negatively to reinforce their projections ("Oh come on, you don't really believe that do you?").

- There is greater interaction between the respondent and the interviewer.

Don't Ask Them to Vote

It is very important in the P.E.T. process that we not ask the respondents to rank the concepts, or to select the three or four they like the best. At this stage we are trying to learn the most important benefits, the ones that will satisfy their needs, and there may be elements from several of the different concepts that must ultimately work together in a completely new concept execution. So if we asked them which is their favorite, how will we know what else they would like included?

This process is similar to building a rock wall. You look at one rock at a time, analyze it, see its good and bad points, then determine where it will best fit. By the time you go through enough rocks you should have a good-looking and sturdy structure. But you might have to go get some new rocks, and throw away some before you achieve the desired effect.

Learning from Rejection

Marketers, researchers, and new product development people must somehow get over the stigma that being rejected is negative. If we are being rejected, there is a reason. And therein lies an opportunity, not a failure.

In new product development work if we just get nods of agreement from our respondents, we haven't learned a thing. They may be nodding to please us, or to get out of the interview early, but they may also be hiding their true feelings from us.

For the P.E.T. strategy it is a happy occasion when someone says "No, that doesn't work for me." Because then we can say "Why?" Quickly followed by "If it doesn't work for you, how would you change it to help it work for you?" When the respondents start answering those questions, we've gone beyond the opinion level, and they begin projecting their attitudes and needs into the situation.

Rejection is our biggest friend because it opens the door for us to start the probing process and then we can get beyond the surface, or conscious, opinions and help them move into more substantative issues. Once we get there we force them to think about exactly what it is that doesn't work. Then they dig into the subconscious levels and project their needs into the environment of the concept board.

Counter Stimulation

The whole issue of counter stimulation is very important to building successful new products. Respondents must be continually challenged on a "why" basis. If they reply "Yeah, that works pretty well" our interviewer must ask "How can it work better? Change it for us, so it will work better for you."

We must continually stimulate our customer respondents by challenging their responses and forcing them to analyze the concepts from several different perspectives. By using counter stimulation techniques they think about more options, and finally help us build a better concept by synthesizing the benefits that are important to them.

The Magic Wand

Another projective technique that works well is to stimulate the respondent to change anything on the concept board that he or she wants to. There are several ways to do this, but our Magic Wand seems to be very effective.

This is a simple technique, but when the respondent reaches a moment of contemplation, we hand him or her a pencil or a nice pen and say "This is really a magic wand, and I'm going to let you use it for a moment. I'd like you to wave this magic wand, and it will change anything on this concept board that you would like to change. Go ahead, try it." Somewhat sheepishly he or she will take the pen, hold it (and usually *not* wave it!), at which point we ask what they changed and record the response.

Your Chance to Become a Copywriter

Another way we inject creativity into the logic of evaluation is offering respondents an opportunity to become a copywriter for a minute. Their "15 minutes of fame."

This is similar to the Magic Wand, but we hand them a pencil and refer them to the back of the concept board, where the copy is taped. We ask them to pretend they are the advertising agency copywriter, and the creative director has just asked them to change anything they want to in the copy. It's always interesting to see what they change, and why.

Wave Series Ideation

This is an important step in the P.E.T. strategy. Once we have completed an entire research step, be it focus groups or individual interviews, we reconvene for a review. We analyze our findings to date, discuss what we've learned, then begin to modify the concept boards based on those findings.

Some boards are modified, some are deleted, and some are added. And a lot survive unscathed. But every board is reviewed and scrutinized against our findings for each target audience and hard decisions are made about the development of each board. We even review our objectives, and any other consideration, just to make sure we are still on track.

Then we start the interviewing process all over again. We'll do the same type of research, using fresh and different respondents, of course. We always try to minimize respondent bias at this time, and using the same ones could introduce an unwanted bias. They've seen it once, they are likely bringing a bias to the next session.

By doing this wave series ideation process, we are continually gaining new insight. We are always learning new things, and synthesizing them to make them better. Just like the rock wall, above, we keep looking for different and better elements to evolve more effective concepts.

Evolve Winning Concepts

The Perception Expansion Theory process methodically revises, changes, and evolves new elements, and reassembles them into new product concepts that become winners. The P.E.T. strategy works, and has resulted in more new product winners than losers.

It just makes sense. It's like building a house or even a rock wall. Just take one step at a time, and don't be reluctant to say no, that doesn't work. And keep your respondents working for you by breaking the opinion barrier and projecting their attitudes and needs into your marketing successes.

CHAPTER
10

Other Types of Qualitative Research

It is the opinion of the author that while quantitative research is very important to the marketing process, its proper role should follow concept development. Concept development is a psychological process, dealing with feelings, emotions, and attitudes. While we can quantify opinions, as is done on a daily basis with opinion polls for political candidates, issues research, and so on, opinions should not be considered in concept development. Therefore, our focus in this book is on qualitative research methods.

While the Perception Expansion Theory has its own research process, other types of qualitative research can also be helpful, particularly for the input stage, to gather additional qualitative data. These are widely used to gather psychographic data, but not to evolve new product concepts.

Early Psychographic Segmentation

As a review of our discussion in Chapter 2, recall that psychographics help us better understand our customers' potential motivations for purchasing our products. As Jack Haskins states (Haskins 1993, pp. 35–37):

> Psychographics provide insight into consumer motivation by analyzing such variables as personality type, political preference, lifestyle, interests, and personal and social aspirations. In 1971, William Wells and Douglas Tigert introduced the notion of attitudes, interests, and opinions (AIO) as a basis for segmenting market groups.

Exhibit 10.1

Items from Early Activities, Interests, and Opinion Studies:

Precursors of Psychographic Segmentation

Price Conscious

I shop a lot for "specials."

I find myself checking the prices in the grocery store even for small items.

I usually watch the advertisements for announcements of sales.

A person can save a lot of money by shopping around for bargains.

Fashion Conscious

I usually have one or more outfits that are of the very latest style.

When I must choose between the two I usually dress for fashion, not for comfort.

An important part of my life and activities is dressing smartly.

I often try the latest hairstyles when they change.

Child Oriented

When my children are ill in bed I drop most everything else in order to see to their comfort.

My children are the most important thing in my life.

I try to arrange my home for my children's convenience.

I take a lot of time and effort to teach my children good habits.

Compulsive Housekeeper

I don't like to see children's toys lying about.

I usually keep my house very neat and clean.

I am uncomfortable when my house is not completely clean.

Our days seem to follow a definite routine, such as eating meals at a regular time.

Dislikes Housekeeping

I must admit I really don't like household chores.

I find cleaning my house an unpleasant task.

I enjoy most forms of housework. (Reverse scored)

My idea of housekeeping is "once over lightly."

Seamstress

I like to sew and frequently do.

I often make my own or my children's clothes.

You can save a lot of money by making your own clothes.

I would like to know how to sew like an expert.

Homebody

I would rather spend a quiet evening at home than go out to a party.

I like parties where there is lots of music and talk. (Reverse scored)

I would rather go to a sporting event than a dance.

I am a homebody.

Community Minded

I am an active member of more than one service organization.

I do volunteer work for a hospital or service organization on a fairly regular basis.

I like to work on community projects.

I have personally worked in a political campaign or for a candidate or an issue.

Credit User

I buy many things with a credit card or a charge card.

I like to pay cash for everything I buy. (Reverse scored)

It is good to have charge accounts.

To buy anything, other than a house or a car, on credit is unwise. (Reverse scored)

Continued

Sports Spectator

I like to watch or listen to baseball or football games.

I usually read the sports page in the daily paper.

I thoroughly enjoy conversations about sports.

I would rather go to a sporting event than a dance.

Cook

I love to cook.

I am a good cook.

I love to bake and frequently do.

I am interested in spices and seasonings.

Self-Confident

I think I have more self-confidence than most people.

I am more independent than most people.

I think I have a lot of personal ability.

I like to be considered a leader.

Self-Designated Opinion Leader

My friends or neighbors often come to me for advice.

I sometimes influence what my friends buy.

People come to me more often than I go to them for information about brands.

Information Seeker

I often seek out the advice of my friends regarding which brand to buy.

I spend a lot of time talking with my friends about products and brands.

My neighbors or friends usually give me good advice on what brands to buy in the grocery store.

New Brand Tryer

When I see a new brand on the shelf I often buy it just to see what it's like.

I often try new brands before my friends and neighbors do.

I like to try new and different things.

Satisfied with Finances

Our family income is high enough to satisfy nearly all our important desires.

No matter how fast our income goes up we never seem to get ahead. (Reverse scored)

I wish we had a lot more money. (Reverse scored)

Canned Food User

I depend on canned food for at least one meal a day.

I couldn't get along without canned foods.

Things just don't taste right if they come out of a can. (Reverse scored)

Dieter

During the warm weather I drink low calorie soft drinks several times a week.

I buy more low calorie foods than the average housewife.

I have used Metrecal or other diet foods at least one meal a day.

Financial Optimist

I will probably have more money to spend next year than I have now.

Five years from now the family income will probably be a lot higher than it is now.

Wrapper

Food should never be left in the refrigerator uncovered.

Leftovers should be wrapped before being put into the refrigerator.

Wide Horizons

I'd like to spend a year in London or Paris.

I would like to take a trip around the world.

Continued

> **Arts Enthusiast**
>
> I enjoy going through an art gallery.
>
> I enjoy going to concerts.
>
> I like ballet.
>
> ---------
>
> Source: William Wells and Douglas Tigert, "Activities, Interests and Opinions," reprinted in "Advertising Research Classics," *Journal of Advertising Research*, September 1982, pp. 30–38.

VALS

The next major attempt to refine psychographic evaluation of customers was initiated by Stanford Research Institute (SRI) in 1978 with their Values and Lifestyles System (VALS). This was the first attempt to quantify psychographic qualities to assist marketers. SRI grouped the population into several categories, according to their personality types. Haskins describes the groupings (p. 38–40) as:

Actualizers

Actualizers are successful, sophisticated, active, "take-charge" people with high self-esteem and abundant resources. They are interested in growth and seek to develop, explore, and express themselves in a variety of ways—sometimes guided by principle, and sometimes by a desire to have an effect, to make a change. Image is important to Actualizers, not as evidence of status or power, but as an expression of taste, independence, and character. Actualizers are among the established and emerging leaders in business and government, yet they continue to seek challenges . . . .

Principle-Oriented

Principle-oriented consumers seek to make their behavior consistent with their views of how the world is or should be.

Fulfilleds are mature, satisfied, comfortable, reflective people who value order, knowledge, and responsibility. Most are well educated and in, or recently retired from, professional occupations. They are content with their careers, families, and station in life; well-informed about the world and national events; and alert to opportunities to broaden their knowledge. Their leisure activities tend to center around their homes . . . .

Believers are conservative, conventional people with concrete beliefs based on traditional, established codes: family, church, community, and the nation. Many Believers express moral codes that are deeply rooted and literally interpreted. They follow established routines, organized in large part around their homes, families, and social or religious organizations to which they belong. As consumers, they are conservative and predictable, favoring American products and established brands. Their education, income, and energy are modest but sufficient to meet their needs.

Status-Oriented

Status-oriented consumers have or seek a secure place in a valued social setting . . . .

Achievers are successful career and work-oriented people who like to, and generally do, feel in control of their lives. They value structure, predictability, and stability over risk, intimacy, and self-discovery. They are deeply committed to their work and their families . . . .

Strivers seek motivation, self-definition, and approval from the world around them. They are striving to find a secure place in life. Unsure of themselves and low on economic, social, and psychological resources, Strivers are deeply concerned about the opinions and approval of others. Money defines success for Strivers, who don't have enough of it, and often feel that life has given them a raw deal. Strivers are sensitive to the tastes and preferences of the persons with whom they live and socialize. They may try to emulate those who own more impressive possessions, but what they wish to obtain is often beyond their reach.

Action-Oriented

Action-oriented consumers like to affect their environment in tangible ways. Makers do so primarily at home and at work, Experiencers in the wider world. Both types tend to become intensely involved in their activities.

Experiencers are young, vital, enthusiastic, impulsive, and rebellious. They seek variety and excitement, savoring the new, the offbeat, the risky. Still in the process of formulating life values and patterns of behavior, they quickly become enthusiastic about new possibilities but are equally quick to cool. At this stage in their lives, they are politically uncommitted, uninformed, and highly ambivalent about what they believe . . . .

Makers are practical people who have constructive skills and value self-sufficiency. They live within a traditional context of family, practical work, and physical recreation and have little interest in what lies outside that context. Makers experience the world by working on it—building a house, raising children, fixing a car, or canning vegetables—and have sufficient skill, income, and energy to carry out their projects successfully . . . .

Strugglers

Strugglers' lives are constricted. With limited economic, social, and emotional resources, and often in poor health, Strugglers experience the world as pressing and difficult. Because they are so limited, they show no evidence of a strong self-orientation, but are focused on meeting the urgent needs of the present moment. Strugglers are cautious consumers. They represent a very modest market for most products and services, but are loyal to favorite brands.

VALS is a rather interesting analysis of our population, and one that is widely used for positioning and marketing established brands, and for input in the development of new products. As stated above, VALS can be a valuable tool for generating insight for new product development, prior to concept development. By identifying potential psychographic targets, the concept development can be more focused.

DAGMAR

Another popular psychographic/demographic analysis, mostly used for established brands, is Designing Advertising Goals for Measured Advertising Results (DAGMAR, Colley). While this is basically an analysis of advertising positioning for existing brands, it serves as an excellent checklist for new product introductions.

Review the grids in Exhibit 10.2 with the thought of using DAGMAR to prepare the introductory advertising positioning of new products. You'll agree that it can be an excellent guideline for your new product introduction.

Yankelovich Monitor

Daniel Yankelovich founded *Monitor*, which was another attempt to quantify various lifestyles throughout the population. Monitor was based on several thousand personal, telephone and mailed questionnaire interviews with a sample base that was statistically balanced to reflect a cross-section of our population.

The study identified lifestyle groupings similar to the later VALS study, and was truly a pioneering effort to give some better understanding of psychographic clustering. The Monitor study was syndicated to hundreds of marketing organizations, large and small, throughout the U.S., and even internationally.

The advantage of Monitor was that it was one of the earlier attempts at market segmentation based on a psychographic profile of consumers.

Exhibit 10.2

DAGMAR Grids

To what extent does the advertising aim at closing an *immediate sale*?

1. Perform the complete selling function (take the product through all the necessary steps toward a sale)?

2. Close sales to prospects already partly sold through past advertising efforts ("Ask for the order" or "clincher" advertising)?

3. Announce a special reason for "buying now" (price, premium, etc.)?

4. *Remind* people to buy?

5. Tie in with some special buying event?

6. Stimulate impulse sales?

OTHER TASKS:

	SCALE OF IMPORTANCE					
	Not Important			Very Important		
	0	1	2	3	4	5
1.						
2.						
3.						
4.						
5.						
6.						

Does the advertising aim at *near-term* sales by moving the prospect, step by step, closer to a sale (so that when confronted with a buying situation the customer will ask for, reach for, or accept the advertised brand)?

7. Create awareness of existence of product or brand?

8. Create "brand image" or favorable emotional disposition toward the brand?

9. Implant information or attitude regarding benefits and superior features of brand?

10. Combat or offset competitive claims?

11. Correct false impressions, misinformation, and other obstacles to sales?

12. Build familiarity and easy recognition of package or trademark?

OTHER TASKS:

	SCALE OF IMPORTANCE					
	Not Important			Very Important		
	0	1	2	3	4	5
7.						
8.						
9.						
10.						
11.						
12.						

Continued

Does the advertising aim at building a "long-range consumer franchise?"

13. Build confidence in company and brand which is expected to pay off in years to come?

14. Build customer demand which places company in stronger position in relation to its distribution (not at the "mercy of the marketplace")?

15. Place advertiser in position to select preferred distributors and dealers?

16. Secure universal distribution?

17. Establish a "reputation platform" for launching new brands or product lines?

18. Establish brand recognition and acceptance which will enable the company to open up new markets (geographic, price, age, sex)?

	SCALE OF IMPORTANCE					
	Not Important			Very Important		
	0	1	2	3	4	5
13.						
14.						
15.						
16.						
17.						
18.						

OTHER TASKS: _____

Specifically, how can advertising contribute toward increased sales?

19. Hold present customers against the inroads of competition?

20. Convert competitive users to advertiser's brand?

21. Cause people to specify advertiser's brand instead of asking for product by generic name?

22. Convert non-users of the product type to users of product and brand?

23. Make steady customers out of occasional or sporadic customers?

24. Advertising new uses of the product?

	SCALE OF IMPORTANCE					
	Not Important			Very Important		
	0	1	2	3	4	5
19.						
20.						
21.						
22.						
23.						
24.						

25. Persuade customers to buy larger sizes of multiple units?

26. Remind users to buy?

27. Encourage greater frequency or quantity of use?

OTHER TASKS:

_____

	SCALE OF IMPORTANCE					
	Not Important			Very Important		
	0	1	2	3	4	5
25.						
26.						
27.						

Does the advertising aim at some specific step which leads to a sale?

28. Persuade prospect to write for descriptive literature, return a coupon, enter a contest?

29. Persuade prospect to visit a showroom, ask for a demonstration?

30. Induce prospect to sample the product (trial offer)?

OTHER TASKS:

_____

	SCALE OF IMPORTANCE					
	Not Important			Very Important		
	0	1	2	3	4	5
28.						
29.						
30.						

How important are "supplementary benefits" of end-use advertising?

31. Aid sales force in opening new accounts?

32. Aid sales force in getting larger orders from wholesalers and retailers?

33. Aid sales force in getting preferred display space?

34. Give sales force an entrée?

35. Build morale of company sales force?

36. Impress the trade (causing recommendation to their customers and favorable treatment to sales force)?

OTHER TASKS:

_____

	SCALE OF IMPORTANCE					
	Not Important			Very Important		
	0	1	2	3	4	5
31.						
32.						
33.						
34.						
35.						
36.						

Continued

Is it a task of advertising to impart information needed to consummate sales and build customer satisfaction?

37. "Where to buy it" advertising?

38. "How to use it" advertising?

39. New models, features, package?

40. New prices?

41. Special terms, trade-in offers, etc.?

42. New policies (guarantees, etc.)?

OTHER TASKS:

	SCALE OF IMPORTANCE					
	Not Important			Very Important		
	0	1	2	3	4	5
37.						
38.						
39.						
40.						
41.						
42.						

To what extent does the advertising aim at building confidence and good will for the corporation among:

43. Customers and potential customers?

44. The trade (distributors, dealers, retail salespeople)?

45. Employees and potential employees?

46. The financial community?

47. The public at large?

OTHER TASKS:

	SCALE OF IMPORTANCE					
	Not Important			Very Important		
	0	1	2	3	4	5
43.						
44.						
45.						
46.						
47.						

Specifically what kind of images does the company wish to build?

48. Product quality, dependability?

49. Service?

50. Family resemblance of diversified products?

51. Corporate citizenship?

52. Growth, progressiveness, technical leadership?

OTHER TASKS:

_____

SCALE OF IMPORTANCE					
Not Important			Very Important		
0	1	2	3	4	5
48.					
49.					
50.					
51.					
52.					

Source: Russell H. Colley, *Defining Advertising Goals for Measured Advertising Results,* Association of National Advertisers, Inc., rev. and exp. Solomon Dutka (Lincolnwood, Ill: NTC Business Books), pp. 80–88.

Widely used by consumer marketers, it also offered business-to-business organizations a special consulting service in which the Yankelovich staff would interpret data and identify marketing opportunities.

Also an advantage for Monitor was that it was an annual survey, massive in scope, and, seemingly, highly interpretive of the various lifestyle groupings identified by Yankelovich. By being an annual survey Monitor could track changes, and subtle shifts, and provide an early indication to marketers of changing lifestyles.

For example, Monitor picked up the fitness trend early on, and predicted that it would not be a fad, but a definite change in our lifestyles. It also identified an early concern for our environment, opening opportunities for both consumer and business-to-business marketers. One of the findings with the most significant impact, perhaps, was the early indication that people were running out of time each day, because there were just too many new demands on their time. So Yankelovich started talking about developing products and services which would help people save time.

The Yankelovich staff would make major presentations to their subscribers (they called them "clients") each year with their overall findings. They would then be available on a consulting basis to help interpret the data and provide more insight into what they thought the trends implied for their client's particular industry or market segment.

Monitor is a highly respected service and has been used in the marketing business for many years. Today, Monitor and VALS are still the undisputed leaders in psychographic research.

Why the Perception Expansion Theory Is Important to New Product Research

The first step in any new product or market definition study is to review existing secondary data—those data that already exist. This is called "desk top research," and is usually a thorough search for any data that might be appropriate for the product category of interest. Some of the more commonly used studies of this type include the following:

- VALS
- Yankelovich Monitor
- Proper Reports
- A.C. Nielsen
- Sales & Marketing Management
- Starch
- Simmons
- Statistical Abstract of the United States

The local business library is also an effective resource that is often overlooked. There are many catalogs, trade association directories, government publications, and other endless sources of information. All of these sources help you to understand the marketplace.

The Problem

The problem with all of these data, is that they show us where the market was at a given time, the time the survey was done. These are static reports that are probably outdated by the time they reach our desks, but they do provide some insight as to how things were at that time.

Much of these data are now available on the Internet, thus bypassing many traditional distribution sources. But the data are still subject to the delays of data collection, processing, interpretation, analysis, and report preparation. Some time is saved in the distribution process, but probably not enough to be meaningful.

All of these studies say to us "let's understand where we are." Certainly, it is important for us to understand where we are, as we can't successfully develop new products without that knowledge. However, at some point we have to move on, to develop products for a new and emerging customer, with new needs that change rapidly—even too rapidly to be picked up by our syndicated services.

Most of this research, properly interpreted, provides us with an overview of where we might find opportunities. It is not dynamic or particularly projective. It cannot lead us to find new places, only record where we've been.

The Perception Expansion Theory Advantage

An artist friend of mine calls realistic art, such as landscapes, portraits, pastoral settings, and so on "sofa art." She says, "You may as well hang a photograph there, because that art is not designed to take you to new places. Whereas abstract art, and other art forms, can take you to new dimensions."

The P.E.T. process is designed to take you to new dimensions. We need the P.E.T. process to begin where most qualitative research leaves us. P.E.T. should be used to supplement these other studies, and to build on them. P.E.T. is the abstract art of qualitative research. Just as some art can deliver us to a new destination, so can P.E.T.

Most of the appropriate qualitative research is reviewed during the initial input session. These data are reviewed exhaustively, and it ends there. Reports are written and endless memos analyze "areas of opportunity" and "suggested further action." All are important, but this research review has not taken us to new places.

P.E.T. theory begins after the initial input session, after all of the other secondary data have been reviewed, analyzed, and reported. Then we go new places. With the immersion and exploratory steps we actually begin to apply the data learned from the original qualitative step.

This theory is still qualitative research, just as photos and abstract art are *art*. But P.E.T. has the capability of helping us move ahead, of applying the findings of the syndicated studies to create *successful new products*. P.E.T. has the capacity of provoking our creativity, of leading us to new dimensions. We can find out we are with the other qualitative studies and the Internet. What we need are strategies and theories to take us beyond.

They say: Let's understand where we are. We say: Here's where we can go with it.

CHAPTER 11

Business-to-Business Opportunities

Business-to-business new product development offers some of the best opportunities for successful marketing. There are several reasons for this, which we will explore.

Business-to-business marketing includes creating new products to be directed at retailers, wholesalers, distributors, and others in the retail chain. It also includes products to be directed toward professionals, such as doctors and lawyers, or to industrial outlets such as manufacturers or processors.

These people in business buy or analyze and specify products or services for use in their own organizations. These organizations might include retail or commercial businesses, agricultural firms, government, even entertainment. They purchase a wide variety of products for their enterprises. We'll take a closer look at these below.

Major New Product Opportunities

While formal and active business-to-business new product programs are often overlooked by many marketing professionals, we believe there is a major opportunity within the category to be preemptive in new product programs. The needs of the business-to-business marketer are so diverse, different for each customer category, that the creative new products manager can capitalize on many different opportunities rather quickly, and relatively inexpensively.

The business-to-business marketer usually has several different customer categories for their products. If they currently are only serving one, they have an immediate opportunity to create new products, or reposition existing ones, to reach new customer bases. This provides an enormous opportunity for new products, as each of the customers is buying the same product, but for different applications. Each of the customers has a different set of needs, with different applications, and all want the same product, perhaps slightly modified to fulfill their personal application needs.

For example, if you are selling lighting, the globes and fixtures, you have many different potential customers. Everyone in business needs lighting, even coal miners and mushroom farmers. Exhibit 11.1 shows how you could analyze your potential customer base, and how the potential new product customer base would be identified.

The list in Exhibit 11.1 is not intended to be exhaustive, rather to give an indication of the many new product opportunities available to one organization in the lighting business. The same analysis would be applicable to any other industry.

The main point is that the company is manufacturing and selling lighting fixtures. With little or no modification, the same fixtures can be marketed to a variety of companies for many different applications.

Your Customers Are the Key

There is a simple analysis you can follow to guide your initial thinking in terms of serving your customers with new product opportunities. It seems simple at first, but it is surprising how many times one or both of these steps is overlooked:

Know Your Customers

Most of us think we know our customers well, know their habits, their needs, even their products. Remember, your customers are buying from you for one reason only. They are buying from you because you are currently satisfying their needs. Your utility to them will last as long as you continue to fulfill that function. So you'd better know them very well, and where they are headed with their businesses.

Exhibit 11.1

Hypothetical Lighting Industry
New Product Development Model

Industry	Potential Applications	Customer Base
Retail	Supermarkets Department stores Boutiques Specialty outlets	Managers Architects Designers Contractors Distributors Customers
Construction— Industrial	Warehouses Manufacturing plants Assembly plants Large structures Highways	Designers Architects Contractors Distributors End-users
Construction— Commercial	Office buildings Strip malls Motels Restaurants Schools	Designers Architects Contractors Potential tenants Distributors
Construction— Residential	Apartments Homes Storage units	Architects Contractors Distributors
Entertainment	Movie theaters Performing theaters Auditoriums Exterior stages	Lighting engi- neers Interior designers Contractors Performers
Government	Buildings Storage units Roadways Security lighting Military applications Airfields	Architects Contractors Specifiers Purchasing agents Dept. of Defense

Industry	Potential Applications	Customer Base
Professional	Physicians	FDA
	Lawyers	Designers
	Hospitals	Medical
Administrators		
		Contractors
		Lawyers
		Physicians
Agricultural	Farms	Farmers
	Greenhouses	Architects
	Drying towers	Contractors
Industrial	Automotive	Engineers
	Electronic	Computer users
	Aviation	Plant managers
	Hazardous plants	Specifiers
	Stadiums	Contractors
	Parking areas	Distributors

Develop a Problem-Solving Relationship

Try to get to know your customers well enough that they will begin to share your problems with you. Once you can reach that stage, they will begin to share with you some of their needs. Try to make them partners with you, not just customers—build an element of trust.

Identify the special problems they face with *their* customers in their particular marketing categories. Do they dominate the category? What are their marketing objectives, their long-term growth plans? What are their goals in terms of new product development?

Help them identify the primary problems facing their business. Is technology a problem, are they having supplier problems, is labor a problem for them? And what about *their* customers' problems? How can you help them solve their customers' problems?

Treat your customers as partners. Your success with your customers is directly related to how well you can help them solve their problems. Help them create new products, by creating them for them. Help them identify their own needs, as well as the needs of their customers. This principle is quite well illustrated in Chapter 12. We look at how Eastman Kodak (Chemicals Division) did exactly that, and solved a lot of problems for everyone.

Repositioning

When an organization sells its products for several different applications, this is referred to as repositioning the product. This is actually an extension of new product development, in that the same principles apply in terms of identifying needs and *creating a new concept* to fulfill those needs. Note the emphasis—we are creating a new concept, not a new product. The existing product may have to be modified a bit, but we are not starting from scratch.

Essentially, we are trying to create the perception of a new product by giving it new or additional benefits to make it fulfill the needs of additional customers. We can accomplish this by (1) modifying the *product* to fit the needs of our customers, or by (2) modifying the *perception* of the product's benefits to fulfill those needs. Since we know that perception is reality, we have actually created a new product.

The process of repositioning a product is almost exactly the same as creating a new product concept. The steps outlined in Chapters 8 and 9 should be followed in repositioning assignments. We are still trying to get beyond opinions and into our customers' attitudes. We are trying to identify their needs, and we are trying to give our products benefits that will fulfill the needs of those customers.

The process remains the same, except that when repositioning existing brands we have more data to work with at the input stage. But everything else in the P.E.T. process should be followed just as in starting without existing products. Just remember to set aside the inherent biases surrounding the brand, which is more difficult to do when starting with an existing and, it is hoped, successful product that has provided a revenue stream for some time.

This being the case, many involved people are very reluctant to start tinkering with the product. However, the old adage of "If it ain't broke, don't fix it" does not apply here. It ain't broke but we're trying to double our pleasure by making it work again, somewhere else, in somebody else's backyard. It will not have an adverse affect on the original product.

During the immersion stage, do a simple modeling exercise like the sample category analysis we provided for the lighting industry. In this sample exercise, we found 39 potential applications. Sure, the company is selling to some of them already, but not all of them. And by simply repositioning their existing products they were able to open up many new potential applications. This is an actual example, and the company's sales increased over 40 percent in two years.

Other New Product Development Advantages

Developing new products in the business-to-business category has other advantages. These affect the alacrity with which we can develop new product concepts, as well as the efficiency and expenses. These advantages include customer clusters, a customer knowledge base, customers' bottom-line orientation and the fact that new product needs are dictated by customers' business objectives.

Customer Clusters

Typically, the customer base for business-to-business marketers is relatively small compared to the giants dealing with the American consumer market. The larger consumer organizations can't possibly personally know consumers, their families, their habits, or even their needs or desires, in most cases.

The electrical manufacturer referenced above probably has a maximum of 100 distributors nationally, accounting for 80 percent of their sales. They know their names, their addresses, their family status, their personal likes and habits. They treat the distributors as partners.

When the author's firm was doing a new product project for this company, the distributors welcomed us to come in and take time to interview them. They were thrilled to be included in the evaluation of new product concepts (during the exploratory stage), although they were not surprised this large electrical manufacturer would include them. That's the type of culture that can exist in business-to-business marketing.

Customer Knowledge Base

These customers, partners, or clients, whichever term you choose, are also very knowledgeable about their products, their own customers, and their principles—in this case, the electric companies they represent. This is a unique advantage for the business-to-business marketer.

The customers are also business people. By and large, they know business principles, they know their products very well, they know who are buying them, what they are paying for them, the last time they bought from them, and any problems that they may have had with one another.

These business customers know how to use data for comparative reasons, and will buy the goods and services that make the most sense for them. But they do it on a rational basis, because they are investing for their companies, and, for the most part, not to satisfy some personal whim.

This is one of the nice things about developing new products for business-to-business marketers. When you involve their customers, e.g., the distributors, that's "where the rubber hits the road!" There is no doubt but that when you break through their opinion barrier and tap into the attitudes, you've struck a gold mine. Once you get past the rhetoric of the latest peer group opinion formation, they contain a wealth of knowledge about the category, their principles, their own customers, and their competitors. And they are more willing to share it than with any other form of marketing. They realize they have nothing to lose and everything to gain.

Bottom-Line Orientation

Business-to-business customers are business people, by definition. With this, they are following the guidelines of strategic planning and a bottom-line orientation of "let's bring it in on time, and on budget." We've seen they are very knowledgeable about the industry, the products, and the key players in the marketplace.

However, there are some drawbacks associated with this. Many of the major hitters in business-to-business marketing are large corporations with layer upon layer of executive talent. However, those layers of talent often create a corporate viscosity that works against rapid change and development.

New Product Needs Dictated by Objectives

Being so knowledgeable and having a bottom-line orientation have a major impact on their new product development programs. The needs change from personal desires and attitudinal orientation, to "what's best for the company?"

However, the needs are still there. And we still must have a firm understanding of those needs, still coming from the attitudinal level, to be able to help our customers. Some of these new needs are likely to center around the following questions:

1. "Can this supplier provide the quality new product stream I need?" Your customers always search for quality levels that are equal to, or better than, those they are currently using. No company wants to admit to lowering their quality standards. They may, however, bring out a line extension, a new product, or reposition an existing brand to lower the price. But they would rarely admit to lowering the quality.

Your opportunity, then, is to show them ways to bring out new products that are as effective as current brands, but at a lower cost. This could be to offer them new ingredients, new formulations or technologies, even new packaging. But show them how you can maintain the same quality, and offer other benefits.

2. "Will this supplier be in business next year?" This is always a concern in new supplier/customer relationships. Particularly if one or the other is newly in business, or relatively unknown. Corporate "right-sizing" has created many new, small, unknown companies, and the more established companies are very concerned about this.

You must employ a very skilled PR person, advertising agency, or outside sales staff to allay fears of financial collapse. And this works both ways. The marketers are just as concerned about the new start-up customer going out of business as the customers are about the new start-up supplier going out of business. Both are very concerned, so provide relief up-front.

3. "Can this supplier provide the ongoing service I need?" Your potential customers have tight production schedules, just as your current customers have. If you develop some exciting new products for them, they need assurances you can deliver. Remember, they have customers too.

Whenever you introduce a new product to them, always assure them of adequate inventories, availability of raw materials, packaging, and all that goes into the supply process. Many marketers are now guaranteeing delivery schedules, with adequate prior ordering commitments.

4. "Will this supplier be discreet with my competition?" One of the greatest fears in business-to-business marketing is supplier discretion. It is such a small world, and everyone knows everyone else. Will my new supplier be discreet with my secrets? How do I know?

All of the legal documents and contracts you can muster will not allay all of their fears. It takes time, a building of trust and confidence, and generating a feeling that you really do want to be partners with them.

5. "How will this new product affect my bottom line?" There is always concern about the bottom line, as discussed above. After all, that's what business is all about.

So show them how you can help them protect their bottom line. Then do it. That's the best reassurance you can provide that you mean business too. Give them creative ways to do it, and make it an ongoing consulting business. Make them look good against that bottom line.

6. "Will this supplier really help solve my problems by delivering the new products they've promised?" Isn't this what it's all about? Don't we create new products and services to help them solve problems? Our job, however, is to convince them that we will, and are, helping them solve problems.

That's precisely why we want to bring them into the loop at the very early stages of an active new product development program. By including them in the earliest stages, the exploratory stage, you not only convince them that you want their input, but you're trying to help them solve problems.

They will appreciate this, and you've alleviated a major obstacle in selling them products in the future. After all, they helped design it, didn't they?

7. "Do I really want to be a partner with this company?" You must continually reassure potential customers that it is O.K. to be a partner with you. After all, you've developed a new product for them, haven't you?

This is probably the most compelling reason to involve them in the initial stages of your new product development process. If we do that correctly, this question is obviated.

8. "How will this decision make me look in the organization?" That's the real bottom line, isn't it? Be certain to reassure your customers on this point.

Developing Successful Products for a Global Community

Mass communication institutions remain predominantly nationalistic in character. However, recent developments with the Internet and the World Wide Web are having tremendous impact:

> Some media organizations do have transnational communication as their primary objective, and others are organized largely towards international audiences. One of the most important origins of the newspaper was the channeling of information about events in Europe (and further afield) through the routes of the postal system, which was then published as news in the commercial centres of the early seventeenth century, especially Amsterdam and London. The most significant examples of international media organizations are still probably the global news and news-film agencies, even though these have a strong national base. Other media with an international task were the numerous radio stations designed to disseminate information and the cultural and political messages of various nation states. This media phenomenon continues, but it hardly counts as mass communication. (McQuail 1994, p. 176)

Today, as we encounter the information age, we are continually dealing with global communication. The Web and the Internet have served to shrink the world even more, and scarcely a day goes by that we don't encounter the effects of global communication on some part of our lives.

Cultural Specificity

In new product development we are constantly dealing with cultural domination, the process in which nationalism, or the protection of national cultures, dominates our assessment of the benefits of new concepts. While the concern over cultural domination lessened a bit during the late 1980s and early 1990s, there are signs of a resurgence in many of the European and Asian cultures as they struggle for political and economic identity.

In recent years the marketing community in the United States has debated the potential bottom-line impact of the specific cultural identity of products and services. Is it more efficient (profitable) to position products in a pan-global manner, or to create culturally specific positionings for each new entry?

Does the savings in media in using a pan-global message offset the potential increased sales by being more culturally specific with your positioning message? An article by Kim Foltz in the venerable *New York Times* a few years ago touched off a debate within the Center for Creative Marketing:

American Express to Try a Pan-European Campaign

American Express will begin a series of innovative commercials in Europe this month that essentially use the same message to sell its credit cards in five countries.

In five countries/cultures, the same message? The article continues:

Many American advertisers have been reluctant to use pan-European campaigns because *they have found it difficult to come up with a single message that will not lose its effectiveness in translation or cause confusion from different cultures.* [Emphasis added]

Precisely our thesis. However, there is no consensus:

Still, marketing experts, like Theodore Levitt, a Harvard Business School professor, have said the best way to market products internationally is to use global campaigns that sell them the same way everywhere.

However, our thesis is that for the most effective communication we must be as specific as possible for the *culture* or *customer* we are trying to reach. The article continues:

> For example, commercials for laundry detergent must have separate strategies for each country. French and German women, who are more career-oriented, have a view of washing clothes that is different from that of the more traditionally family-oriented women in Spain and Italy, agency executives said.

This article really aroused our curiosity, as a "marketing expert" like Ted Levitt, at Harvard, was still teaching the "We (Americans) are always right, and what's good for us is good for the world as well." We didn't buy in to that, finding it a bit too cavalier and presumptuous for today's marketing mix.

We designed our own study, with the help of Eastman Kodak, Chemical Division, to explore the impact of global marketing. Our findings refute Ted Levitt's position, clearly indicating that each culture reacts differently to product positioning, and each culture should be carefully researched prior to attempting new product launches.

Case Study: How Attitudes Affect Product Perceptions

Eastman Kodak (Chemical Division) developed and patented a new technology that had the capability of dispersing many elements, ingredients, pigments, and soon, by utilizing a water-base, rather than a petroleum-base carrier. The chemical explanation for this technology is that AQ Polymers (the code name for the new formulations) are polyesters that are easily dispersed in water or water-ethanol blends.

This technology will allow the delivery of many desired and essential ingredients without the necessity of an oil- or alcohol-base carrier, as was then required. The new technology could deliver sun screens, cosmetic pigments, paint and stain pigments, skin moisturizers, and a lot of other applications, without the need for an oil-base carrier. This would provide the end-user with comparable effectiveness to existing products, but with no oily feeling, no stickiness, no long-lasting "gummy" feeling on the skin, and extremely fast drying and "setting" characteristics.

Eastman Kodak (Chemical Division) does not market to consumers, but prepares and supplies technologies, formulas, and ingredients for consumer marketing organizations such as Unilever, Colgate, or Revlon. For these consumer marketing organizations the potential new product concepts with this new technology are virtually endless. Suffice to say, the technology appears to have many potential product and service applications with both domestic and global implications.

Purpose of the Study

Eastman had attempted preliminary international marketing of the new technology in the United States, the Netherlands, and Germany, but had met with initial resistance because the consumer needs had not been identified or specified for each culture. Their objective with this study was to explore for unidentified and unmet needs in a variety of categories which this new technology might satisfy.

To assure that Eastman was marketing the most effective technology and end-user product benefits to their customers, we used the projective techniques described previously to determine cultural differences that might impact sales. Following the process outlined, we established the following objectives to:

1. Create graphic environmental representations of new product concepts in a variety of marketing categories, representations that offered a variety of product benefits and that could be used to probe for unmet needs

2. Explore how different cultural environments affect the performance and acceptance of new product concepts that are based on a new and unknown technology

3. Explore how cultural perceptual differences might affect the presentation of benefits of the new technology

4. Identify cultural differences that might require different formulations to achieve maximum marketing success

5. Identify unmet needs in the appropriate product categories that might be successfully filled with the AQ Polymers technology

We decided not to use typical *focus* groups or concept tests for this project. These types of research usually have, as an objective, to determine "winning" concepts, and that was not our purpose. This process should be left to the ultimate marketer of the products. Our task is to give the AQ Polymers technology a global marketing definition, and the creation of the final product positioning should be left to those responsible for marketing them. We just wanted to identify the most effective ways to present the new technology.

Our approach needed to use innovative projective techniques to determine the underlying needs, define the products based on those needs, then leave final product positioning to the marketers. As behavioral scientists, we were confronted with the proposition of finding a way to have respondents not just evaluate, but first help generate, applications for this new physical science technology, and in several different cultures.

We reasoned that the most effective technique would be to have both marketers and potential end-users as respondents, and to have them discuss the needs that exist within their own areas of interest—to explore potential applications of this new technology. The use of qualitative projective research seemed most appropriate for this task, but the dilemma remained of how to have respondents help *create* new applications that would fulfill their needs.

Building on McGuire's observations, we reasoned that we must create an environment to facilitate the integration and exploration of new applications. The use of loosely defined graphic stimuli was considered to be appropriate as a beginning, and several illustrated 11 " × 14 " color concept boards were developed to present the most basic attributes. As none of the respondents had any knowledge of the benefits of the AQ Polymers technology, this was believed to be an effective way to present a very basic understanding, or stimulus tool, to begin the exploratory process.

While concept boards have been used in research for many years, a review of literature revealed no data regarding *growing* or *evolving* concept boards in this manner for consumer, industrial or hi-tech product applications. However, we recognized the importance of creating an *exploratory* as opposed to a focused environment if the project were to be successful.

In essence, we were trying to learn from rejection, for if we could break through the opinion barrier and have respondents reject our theses, we could then probe for reasons why our initial positionings were not satisfying or fulfilling their needs. At this point, we reasoned that they would begin sharing their needs and how these graphic environments, or positionings, were not fulfilling them. To fulfill our objectives we conducted in-depth, one-on-one interviews with Eastman's customers, the potential marketers of the new technology, and exploratory groups with the potential end-users, the consumers. Specific target markets were identified, and individuals within the customer groups were selected.

Exploratory idea-generation sessions were conducted to generate known positioning alternatives as starting points. The purpose of this exercise was to generate a broad range of product and marketing concepts that might appeal to potential target market end-users, those that could be identified by Kodak and our research group.

Concepts were purposely designed that *stretched* the known technology to stimulate thought and discussion among respondents. We believe that if respondents reject a particular application as inappropriate, we can then probe their attitudes, having them project or describe what would be more appropriate. We then process these new data, modify the concepts, and add the new ones to the array.

Once the concept boards were finalized, interviews were scheduled with individuals who could possibly have an interest in the new technology, including the following:

- Potential marketers known to have applications for the new technology

- Potential marketers not known to have applications for the new technology

- Trade sources familiar and not familiar with the new technology

- Other sources that may be identified during the interviewing process as significant to the potential use of the applications

Interviews were conducted in *waves*, with personal interviews completed in the first segment. After the initial wave, an analysis of findings and review of the concepts was conducted. Findings were incorporated into some existing boards, new boards were added based on new, previously unidentified needs that emerged, and some boards were deleted as being totally irrelevant. Subsequent interviews were conducted with the new and revised stimuli materials, and similar revisions were made after the interviews were completed.

We attempted to environmentally adapt each board for the United States, the Netherlands, and Germany. Examples of the boards, and specific findings for each new concept follow.

Findings

The concept boards were purposely designed in a nonspecific manner, with several benefits presented in order to judge cultural differences in desired benefits. Our assumption was that if a particular concept was found to be effective in one culture, it did not imply effectiveness in other cultures. Our hypothesis was correct; note the many differences in each board based on the cultural analysis.

Bar Soap. Concept boards for bar soap are shown in Exhibit 12.1. Findings regarding bar soap in each country studied were as follows:

United States:

1. A cream bar providing a soft, smooth feeling is seen as more appropriate for a facial soap rather than for a body soap.

2. Long-lasting fragrance is not appropriate, even a detriment, for a facial soap. Fragrances from soap should not compete with cosmetic fragrances.

3. Soap dish melt-down (dissolving) is a problem, and the promised benefit of "doesn't melt away" is meaningful and desired.

4. Skin that feels soft is important.

Exhibit 12.1

Concept Boards for Bar Soap

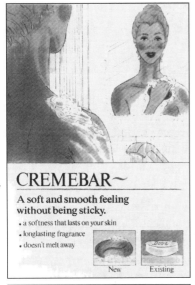

CREMEBAR~

**A soft and smooth feeling
without being sticky.**

- a softness that lasts on your skin
- longlasting fragrance
- doesn't melt away

| New | Existing |

CREME-ZEEP
**EEN ZACHT EN MILDE ZEEP
DIE GEEN PLAKKERIG GEVOEL ACHTERLAAT**

- een blijvend zacht gevoel
  voor je huid
- een blijvende geur
- een zeep die
  niet snel wegsmelt

| CREME | NIVEA |

CREME-SEIFE
**SANFT, MILD UND CREMIG, SIE HINTERLÄßT
KEIN KLEBRIGES GEFÜHL**

- mit einer Zartheit,
  die lange auf der Haut
  fühlbar bleibt
- mit langanhaltemden Duft
- sie löst sich nicht auf,
  bleibt in Form

| CREME | NIVEA |

The Netherlands:

1. Facial and body soaps are different, facial soaps being distinguished by softer, liquid products (milk, lotion, special soaps).

2. Foam (sudsing) is a positive, as it supports the thesis that the product is doing its job. Foam is the *result* of cleaning.

3. Soap is perceived as being hard, and harsh on the skin. The association of a "soft feeling" or "softness" is a difficult juxtaposition.

4. Stickiness isn't associated with cream soap, but long-lasting softness offers a positive advantage.

Germany:

1. Bar soap is rarely used for bathing anymore; gels and liquids are more common to consumers.

2. Perfumed soaps are generally perceived as dermatologically harsh, and not necessary for acceptable product performance.

3. Low price is regarded as very important. Soap is considered to be very functional, with few hedonistic attributes expected.

4. Germans use distinctions of fragrance with body parts, with stronger, high-price fragrances indicating use on the face.

Hair Spray. Concept boards for hair spray are shown in Exhibit 12.2. Findings regarding hair spray in each country studied were as follows:

United States:

1. The alcohol base is widely perceived as a problem for hair, causing abnormally dry hair, split ends, and elimination of protein.

2. A water-base spray would be preferable if it would deliver the same holding characteristics as current sprays.

3. The water-base spray would be preferred due to over-spray problems—consumers don't like the alcohol drifting into their eyes, clothes, or the environment.

The Netherlands:

1. In this humid climate, drying time is important, and there is a perceived contradiction that water would increase the drying time.

2. Dry hair is perceived as a problem, but there is no general association of dryness with the alcohol base of sprays.

3. Split ends are not associated with hair spray, rather with shampoos.

4. Water does not have a positive image for use with cosmetics.

Germany:

1. Water base was readily accepted as environmentally friendly, and was considered a major benefit.

Exhibit 12.2

Concept Boards for Hair Spray

HOLD THAT NATURAL
LOOK FOR YOU
AND YOUR ENVIRONMENT

EASTMAN

NATURA
EEN HAARSPRAY DIE JE HAAR NATUURLIJK
IN VORM HOUDT. GOED VOOR JOU
EN JE OMGEVING: MILIEU-VRIENDELIJK

• een haarspray op waterbasis
  zodat je haar niet uitdroogt
• dus geen gespleten
  haaruiteinden
  meer

EASTMAN

NATURA
SCHONT IHR HAAR AUF NATÜRLICHE
WEISE. IST FREUNDLICH ZU IHNEN UND
IHRER UMWELT

• ein Haarspray auf Wasserbasis
  sodaß Ihr Haar nicht austrocknet
• deshalb keine gespaltenen
  Haarspitzen
  mehr

EASTMAN

2. Consumers accept that a water-base spray would not dry out the hair, but there is no widespread acceptance that hair spray causes dryness.

3. German consumers would like to have professional endorsements (beauty shops, hairdressers) for products of this type—not reflected in the concept board.

4. Water base is associated with a low-price product, perhaps a home-preparation type of product, even a placebo effect.

Shaving Cream. Concept boards for shaving cream are shown in Exhibit 12.3. Findings regarding shaving cream in each country studied were as follows:

Exhibit 12.3

Concept Boards for Shaving Cream

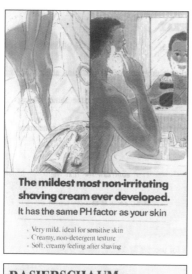

The mildest most non-irritating shaving cream ever developed.

It has the same PH factor as your skin

- Very mild, ideal for sensitive skin
- Creamy, non-detergent texture
- Soft, creamy feeling after shaving

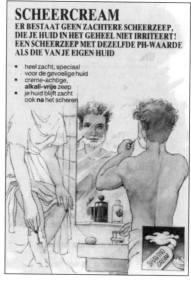

SCHEERCREAM

ER BESTAAT GEEN ZACHTERE SCHEERZEEP, DIE JE HUID IN HET GEHEEL NIET IRRITEERT! EEN SCHEERZEEP MET DEZELFDE PH-WAARDE ALS DIE VAN JE EIGEN HUID

- heel zacht, speciaal voor de gevoelige huid
- creme-achtige, **alkali-vrije** zeep
- je huid blijft zacht ook **na** het scheren

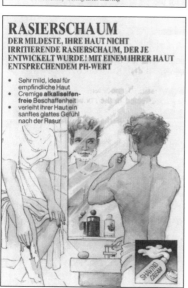

RASIERSCHAUM

DER MILDESTE, IHRE HAUT NICHT IRRITIERENDE RASIERSCHAUM, DER JE ENTWICKELT WURDE! MIT EINEM IHRER HAUT ENTSPRECHENDEM PH-WERT

- Sehr mild, ideal für empfindliche Haut
- Cremige **alkaliseifen-freie** Beschaffenheit
- verleiht ihrer Haut ein sanftes glattes Gefühl nach der Rasur

United States:

1. Shaving is acceptable, and necessary, with American consumers. Women shave their legs frequently, with some using waxing and other epilation methods.

2. Dry skin is a major problem after shaving, for both men and women, and this concept is perceived to be effective for this need.

3. The pH factor is not important—even unknown—and should be replaced with a more direct benefit statement.

4. This product is accepted and desired by both men and women.

The Netherlands:

1. The concept receives a favorable response from men, as a smooth, soft, fresh result is desired.

2. For women, shaving and epilation are two different acts, with different motives and different end results.

3. Effective claims are pH and non-alkali, and non-irritating is also important.

Germany:

1. Men tend to shave daily, but women don't and would not like doing so—epilation is rarely done by shaving.

2. For women, epilation is considered such a "non-feminine" function, there can be no association of the task with a male in the environment. It is not even acceptable to show a lady epilating her legs.

3. The concept of non-irritating does not register—stressing the positive (mildness) is the only way to present the benefits.

4. There has been some negative press about pH factors, so this benefit should be avoided or restated.

Skin Cream. Concept boards for skin cream are shown in Exhibit 12.4. Findings regarding skin cream in each country studied were as follows:

United States:

1. Skin *creams* are associated with facial treatments only. The body is treated with a lotion or an oil.

2. Long-lasting fragrance is not considered a benefit, as women do not want a lotion or cream to compete with other cosmetics fragrances.

3. UV protection is important for a facial cream, not for body lotions or oils.

Exhibit 12.4

Concept Boards for Skin Cream

SKINCREME
A soft creamy skin without the oily feeling.

"Such a soft feeling for my whole body."

• a softness that lasts through the day
• longlasting fragrance
• quickly absorbed
• UV protection - SP25

HUIDCREME GEEFT JE EEN HEERLIJK ZACHTE HUID, ZONDER DAT JE HUID OLIE-ACHTIG AANVOELT

"Super zacht voor m'n hele lichaam"

• een zacht gevoel voor de gehele dag
• een heerlijke geur, die lang aanhoudt
• wordt snel door de huid opgenomen
• beschermt je huid tegen schadelijke UV-stralen met SP 25

HAUTCREME DIE IHNEN EINE SANFTE GESCHMEIDIGE HAUT VERLEIHT OHNE FÜHLBAREN FETTFILM

"Ein so sanftes glattes Gefühl für meinen ganzen Körper"

• eine Sanftheit die den ganzen Tag anhält
• mit langanhaltendem Duft
• wird schnell von der Haut aufgenommen
• schützt Sie vor schädlichen UV-Strahlen durch SP 25

4. There is a wide perception that this product would be better as a sunscreen protector—for protection with no oily feeling.

The Netherlands:

1. Long-lasting softness is a benefit and desired by most consumers, as is the quick absorption.

2. Facial creams should not carry a long-lasting fragrance, for similar reasons as above.

3. A body cream or lotion should provide a refreshing feeling, but carry an aroma only for a maximum of one hour.

4. UV protection is a desired benefit and is being widely accepted in the marketplace with other products.

Germany:

1. Age is a major factor, with younger women preferring the fast absorption, and view the "fat-film" (grease) with disfavor. Older women prefer the fat-film for "glancing" at night.

2. Fragrance is not important, with most German women preferring the nonfragrance creams.

3. UV protection is not necessary—the fewer additives the better.

From the findings generated in the study, we can see that significant cultural differences exist in the perceptions of these new products and the desired benefits. The cultural differences identified are sufficiently strong to warrant major adjustments in formulations, positionings, packaging, and certainly advertising.

Putting It All Together
A Successful Case Study Using the Perception Expansion Theory

The Perception Expansion Theory has been utilized to create many successful new products and services. However, one of the more challenging and rewarding projects was recently completed for the Public Service Company of Colorado.

The Public Service Company of Colorado (PSCo) is a major public utility company supplying power and energy to most of the state of Colorado. The company had been mired in regulatory constraints for years, but recently found itself in a climate of deregulation with an opportunity to explore new marketing areas and create a variety of new products and services.

A management team was assembled to explore various areas of opportunity and decided to explore the needs of the home office worker and telecommuters, among others. The following case study reports on the successful completion of the project.

Background

Public Service Company of Colorado

A project team assembled by management of the Public Service Company of Colorado (PSCo) was desirous of developing estimates of the size and growth of the home office category, and to develop new products and services in response to the unfulfilled needs of the home office workers, which will help PSCo remain competitive and capitalize on this emerging market. The project team elected to seek external counsel to help execute a project to design the optimum new products and services, and thereby fulfill the objectives of the project.

PSCo research identified two major markets for these new products and services, including business-to-business consulting services and products for the home worker.

Business-to-Business Consulting Services

Business-to-business consulting services are designed to help home workers adjust to and create a successful and productive home office environment. This might include analysis of needs, establishing customer service programs, and other needs to be identified.

Products for the Home Office Worker

Products and services for the home office worker would serve at least six identified submarkets, including:

- Full-time self-employed workers
- Telecommuters
- Spillover (full-time employees taking work home with them)
- Small business owners
- Moonlighters
- Part-time self-employed workers

This new product development process must result in developing value-added products and services to keep PSCo innovative and dynamic in an environment of uncertain competitive and government involvement.

Center for Creative Marketing

Center for Creative Marketing (CCM) is a new-product/motivational marketing consulting organization that specializes in assessing appropriate marketplaces and developing processes to capitalize on business development opportunities. As part of our process we identify unfulfilled needs; create, verify, and implement new product and marketing concepts to fulfill those needs; set communication strategies for clients; and determine the most competitive marketing niche for these concepts.

Objectives

Together, we and PSCo evolved a program that has met the following main objectives for PSCo:

1. To identify the unfilled needs and desires of the home office worker, which may or may not be filled by PSCo

2. To identify the needs associated with the telecommuters' offices, which might or might not be filled by PSCo

3. To identify an new line of products and services for residential use in support of the home office worker

4. To create new products and services that will retain and expand the PSCo share of the commercial customer market, which PSCo has determined to be most valuable and at greatest risk

5. To create new products and services in business-to-business *consulting* services that will increase the share of PSCo among the commercial market

Methodology

To accomplish these objectives, CCM undertook an evaluation and design of a marketplace assessment program, which consisted of several steps. As this was an exploratory and design program, PSCo participated in and reviewed the progress of the project at all stages. Our basic process was as follows:

Immersion

An input meeting was held to review the objectives for PSCo, review existing ideas and marketing concepts previously generated by PSCo, and review potential materials and products to be offered by PSCo, appropriate policies and services applicable to customers, and anything else relevant to an exploration of the various objectives.

Ideation

Several brainstorming and concept generation sessions were held by CCM internally, and with PSCo, in which new concept and positioning alternatives were explored. The purpose was to generate a broad range of product and marketing concept alternatives, which might appeal to the home office worker and to the customer groups.

During these sessions new product ideas, new services, new market positionings, and any potentially relevant concept was encouraged. The purpose was to expand our thinking as broadly as possible, to remove mental parameters from existing marketing conditions.

Production

Concept boards were produced that present the various products and product concepts in a graphic benefit statement format, with supporting copy and features included, as necessary. (See Exhibits 13.1–13.5.) These boards were used in interviews as stimuli materials to help respondents project their needs, attitudes, and perceived benefits of new or existing PSCo product alternatives.

These concept boards even represented products or services considered to be on the periphery of PSCo capabilities. The purpose of the boards was to warm up respondents, to get them to discuss their problems or needs, so we could then focus attention on solving their needs with appropriate products or programs.

Exploration

Once the concept boards were finalized and approved by PSCo, CCM undertook the exploration of the various alternatives to develop the most effective combination of marketing elements.

Seven focus groups were conducted between March 20 and 26, 1996. The groups were held in Denver, with 72 individuals who work at home. Six groups were held with home office workers (defined by PSCo), and one group consisted of telecommuters, those employed by a company on a full-time basis but who also work at home at least a few days a month. The groups were "blind," meaning the respondents were not aware of the sponsor. The specific makeup of the respondents was:

- Telecommuters, who work at least one day per week at home as part of their regular work duties and hours: 20
- Self-employed, full-time: 22
- Self-employed, part-time: 11

- Spillover (bring extra work home with them or on call): 14
- Moonlighters (work full-time for outside employer, but with own venture at home): 5

During Phase II of the project, 25 individual in-depth interviews were conducted with business executives involved in evaluating and/or establishing telecommuting programs for employees. These executives report a wide range of numbers of employees working at home, from none to over 20 in some organizations. These were "blind" interviews, in that PSCo was not revealed as the sponsor of the project, so as to eliminate any positive or negative bias toward the results. The interviews were conducted between March 27 and April 30, 1996.

Respondents were selected among several categories from lists provided by PSCo:

- Large business organizations
- Medium-size business organizations
- Small businesses
- Businesses with known interests in telecommuting programs
- Businesses with no known interest in telecommuting programs.

When establishing interviews we first approached the human resources director to determine who had responsibility within the organization to evaluate and establish a telecommuting program. In virtually every case that responsibility was reserved for the human resources director for initial evaluation. Thus, the preponderance of the individual interviews were with the human resources director who was responsible for evaluating and establishing a telecommuting program.

However, once there was a positive evaluation by human resources and approval from department heads, the responsibility to screen for and to select potential telecommuters was passed on to the supervisorial or managerial level within individual departments. Once telecommuters had been selected, the responsibility of determining needs, counseling, and training reverted back to human resources, so the HR director again became important to our interviewing process.

Most of the organizations that had telecommuters report having two to ten currently working at home a few days a week. For example, one organization, the City of Aurora, has one full-time telecommuter; another, Allstate insurance, has two full-time staff telecommuters and many claims adjusters that telecommute several days a month from the field.

General Findings Regarding People Working at Home

Following are the general findings regarding issues of working at home. We asked respondents to tell us what they liked most, and liked least about working in a home environment. The issues listed are generally in order of number of mentions.

Home office workers said they like the following things most about working at home:

- A strong feeling of independence
- Having greater control over their lives, a sense of autonomy
- Flexible hours
- Greater sense of productivity
- No boss
- Privacy
- Fewer interruptions
- Can set your own pace
- A sense of hours worked translating more directly into compensation
- Ability to screen calls
- Less gossip and chitchat
- No office politics
- Greater environmental comfort
- Fewer expenses such as transportation, parking, wardrobe, lunches
- More control to schedule leisure time for recreation, travel
- Able to be with family, kids
- Tax advantages
- No dress code
- Not as much stress
- No rush hour traffic
- No bureaucracy
- A sense of pride
- Can focus on customers and not have to deal with problem coworkers
- Low overhead

Home office workers said they like the following things least about working at home:

- A strong feeling of isolation
- Loneliness
- Lack of face-to-face interaction, collegial support
- Feeling overlooked
- Difficult to obtain information from others
- Lack of networking opportunities
- Difficult to separate work from home
- Household distractions
- Interruptions by family, neighbors
- Missing an element of synergy
- Lack of community with main office
- Lack of motivation
- Lack of accessibility of help
- Too many distractions
- Data transmission is too slow
- Lack of benefits
- Irregular schedule—too easy to work or take breaks
- Lack of income predictability
- Lack of capital
- No easy technical references
- Too much administrative work
- No computer trouble-shooting or software help
- Transporting materials, data from home to office
- Spending 24 hours a day with spouse
- Uses too much personal time
- Sense of guilt for not working hard enough
- Telephone calls
- Solicitors
- Easy to procrastinate
- Hard to get out of the house

- Miss adult communication, intelligent conversation
- Lack of qualified temporary help
- The mess at home

Telecommuters said they like the following things the most:

- Freedom to produce in a less structured environment
- Fewer interruptions
- Saving time
- Convenience
- Support system from main office
- Saving expenses for car, gasoline, parking, lunches
- Availability to the family to help them with things
- Ability to accomplish important tasks without interruptions
- Freedom from the telephone
- Makes job more tolerable
- No commute in heavy traffic
- Greater creativity
- Being in my own environment
- Not having to get dressed for work

Telecommuters said they like the following things the least:

- High expectations of boss
- Long hours
- No distinction between "home time" and "office time"
- Miss being with other people
- Too many interruptions
- Lack of access to technology and files available at the office
- Lack of equipment
- Inability to duplicate data
- Power failures that leave no options
- Not having a computer that is networked to the office
- Ties up the phone
- No self-discipline
- Loss of camaraderie

Concepts for People Working at Home

Following are the findings for the various concept boards presented to respondents during the focus group sessions. These findings result from a projection of respondents' needs during the sessions, and from a recap of their listing the concepts they like most in an individual, unaided ranking. These concepts are listed in order of priority by totaling the number of mentions among all respondents. (Used with permission of the Public Service Company of Colorado.)

Surge Protector

The surge protector with retractable outlets and back-up power received the most mentions, and, due to its obvious popularity, we elected to not show the concept to the last two groups to save time to probe less clear concepts. Some suggested labelling the cords, and said the back-up power should last a minimum of five minutes, and up to one hour. Anticipated price would be between $50 and $200. Possible suppliers would be GE, Sylvania, Westinghouse, and other electrical supply manufacturers. This product should be outsourced, supplied and branded by PSCo.

Home Management System/Utilities Analyses

The home management system with utilities analyses and paying bills on-line was also very popular. Respondents wanted to maintain control over their checkbooks, but paying bills on-line was very intriguing. Providing energy consumption alternatives was an important option, and some wanted an analysis of "home" versus "office" consumption. This should be developed by PSCo, or outsourced to software developers and marketed by PSCo to users directly via direct marketing, perhaps with statement stuffers. Mailing lists can be bought from other utilities, even nationally. Retail distribution could follow at a later time.

A Phone Number That Follows You Everywhere

While there was an immediate feeling that a phone number that "followed" them would make them too accessible and there could be a loss of privacy, most respondents realized this would solve many problems for them. They acknowledged this would be good for people who travel, or spend a lot of time in their cars. However, they would want an on/off option or personal control over where the number rings (cellular, home, FAX, etc.). It is unknown if PSCo has the internal capability to develop this, but it could be licensed to, and partnered with phone companies. (See Exhibit 13.1.)

Exhibit 13.1

Now, a Phone Number That Follows You Everywhere

Wall-Size Monitor

The wall-size monitor without the eyestrain was quite popular, although the immediate reaction was that it must have good resolution. It was seen as being expensive (upwards of $3,000), but worth it if it had multi-use capability for video and TV, a good sound component, and full motion video. Most like the concept of adding white noise and environmental sounds (waves, crackling fire). Likely providers would be Sony, NEC, Zenith. Respondents would expect to buy the monitor with monthly payments, and they would not expect it to be a full wall size—a smaller monitor than illustrated would suffice. This should be outsourced, then marketed by PSCo as part of a home office program, and could later be licensed to other marketers for retail distribution. (See Exhibit 13.2.)

Modular Systems for Homes and Dorms

The modular office systems was a well-received concept, particularly for individuals just starting in a home office environment. Respondents wanted a variety of sizes, from one fitting in a closet to a more elaborate full-office module. They want the units to be on casters so they can be moved from one location to another, or pulled away from a wall for service or equipment replacement. Some believed the modules should be available with complete computer installations, with choices of equipment, and others wanted to be able to buy the cabinetry and install their own equipment. Most believed the units should be closeable, and they are seen as being good for dorms and small apartments. Some questioned the flexibility and expansion issues, wanting them to be expandable when new equipment is added. Likely providers would be Home Depot, CompUSA, telephone companies. Costs were estimated to be from $2,000 to $10,000. This should be outsourced for both cabinetry and hardware, and marketed by PSCo as part of the home office program. It could then be licensed exclusively, or distributed to large retail chains. (See Exhibit 13.3.)

Software to Help You Establish Networks

Network-establishing software is not usable for everyone, particularly small or independent business owners, but very appropriate and appreciated by many with larger organizations. This must have a voice component, video, and instant feedback. It is seen as a good tool for respondents in remote locations, and an excellent tool for editing documents by several people simultaneously, or for obtaining input by several people. Only a few respondents had any experience with similar systems. This should be outsourced for software development and marketed by PSCo as part of the H-O-W program. Then it could be marketed through retail distribution by software distributors. (See Exhibit 13.4.)

Exhibit 13.2

New Monitors without the Strain

Smart Systems

The smart systems concept was so popular we elected not to further evaluate it in the last two groups to save time for more in-depth evaluation of other concepts. It is seen as being a good tool for monitoring utility costs and saving money. Some were skeptical that it would work with forced air heating, and it must be easy to program and to understand.

Exhibit 13.3

Space Saving Modular Systems
for Homes–Dorms

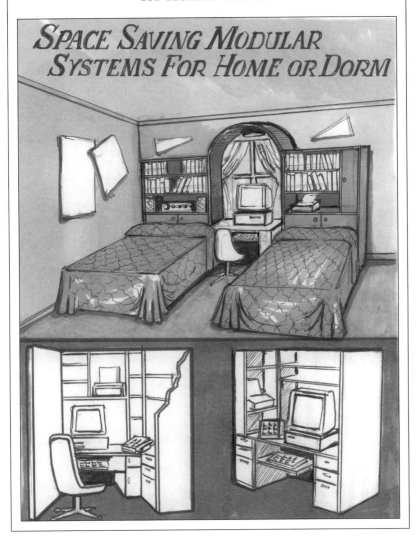

Respondents assume there will be no rewiring and that it will be tamper proof. If this cannot be developed internally, it should be quickly outsourced to electronic product developers, and definitely marketed by PSCo, via direct marketing at first, then through retail distribution. (See Exhibit 13.5.)

Exhibit 13.4

Software to Help You Establish Networks

Remote Environment Control

Respondents liked the convenience for security, for controlling the home while they are not there or as they are returning to the home. It must be easy to program, and ideally have VCR programming capabilities and an alarm system. It is seen as good for people with irregular schedules (to

Exhibit 13.5

Smart Systems

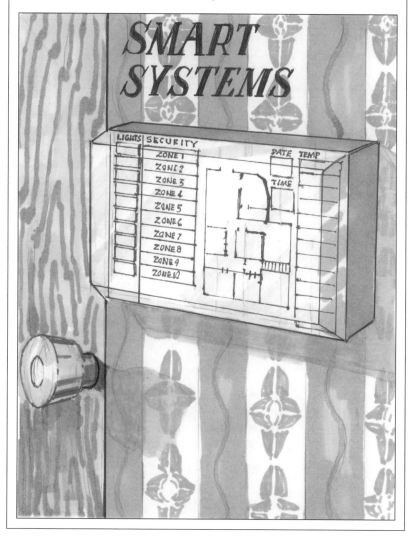

unlock doors for kids, for example), but would need a confirmation of commands. Providers would be security systems, Radio Shack, AT&T, PSCo, and Honeywell. Respondents would expect to pay up to $30 a month for the system. This should be outsourced for development, then marketed by PSCo via direct marketing at first, then distributed to retail outlets.

Modem for Cordless and Cellular Phones

A modem for cordless and cellular phones was seen as a very useful tool, especially for those who travel and use cell phones a lot. E-mail compatibility would be good, and respondents want to be able to download to a printer and have storage for FAX. Receiving capability would be excellent. They would be willing to pay $200 to $500 for this. PSCo should outsource development, then market as part of the H-O-W program via direct marketing. Once that market begins to reach saturation, retail distribution can be undertaken to electronic outlets.

Newsletter

The newsletter concept is seen as being very useful, particularly for the start-up home office worker. It should be available on-line, with hard copy available on request. Many respondents would prefer a general newsletter regarding home office issues, others believed it should be industry specific. Some believed stock quotations would also be useful. They would be willing to pay $5 to $15 for a general information newsletter, and up to $40 to $50 a month if it contained stock quotations, legal and accounting information. They would also like to see a concise summary with each issue.

This can be developed by PSCo rather quickly, then marketed to other regions by direct marketing.

A Uniform Power Supply for Circuits

Uniform power supply is a major need for the home office worker, mentioned 12 times by respondents. This concept and two others answer that need. This concept is not seen being as practical as the surge protector with back-up power because most respondents perceive this would necessitate a rewiring of their homes. This would, however, be excellent in new home construction, and if it could be installed at the circuit box without rewiring the existing home. They expect the unit to include a service contract and to cost from $600 to $1,000, which could be paid cash up front or in monthly installments. This should definitely be developed and marketed by PSCo, first as part of the H-O-W program, later to general markets.

A New Service to Help Telecommuters and Their Families Overcome the Complications of Telecommuting

There is a strong need for a consulting service to help the new home office worker establish and adjust to working at home. This ranges from equipment selection to dealing with the Internet, software, and mental preparation. Respondents recognize a need because they have experienced it and know the complications. They would like this in personal consultation or in a seminar format, and would expect to pay $100 to $200 for the service. This should be marketed by a socio-environmental group, but could be included as part of the H-O-W program, but not under the PSCo name.

Reliable Power

Again, back-up power is a critical issue due to frequent power outages. This concept is seen as very effective, very desirable, and very expensive. Respondents believed retrofitting a home would be prohibitively expensive, but could be affordable if no rewiring is involved; it is an excellent idea for new homes. Health needs might justify the expense. They see this as fitting between the circuit box and the individual circuits, and being supplied by Westinghouse, GE, or the circuit box manufacturers. PSCo could, and probably should, develop and market this concept. If it can be retrofit at a reasonable cost, that would be ideal. Otherwise, it should be developed and marketed to contractors as a value-added product in new homes.

Home Office On-Line Service and Support

While some respondents enjoy taking a break from the home office and shopping, most expressed a need for a courier service that could repair equipment, deliver low-level office supplies such as copy paper or FAX paper. They would expect a quick turnaround, probably within one hour, and they would pay no more than 10 percent over retail rates for the merchandise, or buy a service contract for $10 to $15 per month. While this could be developed by PSCo or licensed to a packager, it should not be marketed under the PSCo name. More appropriate names are available.

Use Consultants to Help Gain Maximum Utility and Security Support

Home office workers have a need for security support. They have insurance needs for equipment and software, and would like to have affordable health insurance offered. There is a desire for a home office worker "association" to establish buying co-ops, insurance, legal and accounting benefits. This could be offered on an annual contract basis with monthly payments and no large up-front payment. This should be licensed to, and packaged by, an individual or organization familiar with these issues. Development and brand name is not appropriate for PSCo.

Administrative and Management System

The concept of an administrative and management system was popular with the home office workers that owned their own businesses. There is a need for more rapid transfer of data, billing, and inventory information. There is some concern about software compatibility, but there is a need, and this software fulfills the need. This is available, but not for the home office worker, only for large companies. Security is an issue, as the H-O-W does not want clients or suppliers having access to their confidential data. This should be outsourced to a software developer, then marketed by PSCo as part of the H-O-W program. Again, retail distribution should be considered after saturation of the home office workers.

Satellite Meeting Rooms

A surprising late entry, only shown to two groups but showing a lot of strength, is satellite meeting rooms. This board, originally designed for the executive interviews, played very well with the home office worker. There are needs for the telecommuter and the H-O-W to be able to access working areas and equipment outside the home. This will facilitate meetings, teleconferencing, and other "group" activities. Locations would be restaurants, airports, and other public meeting places. This should be outsourced for design and development. It could then be licensed, with a healthy license fee, to sales and distribution companies in the top markets nationally for marketing and installation to appropriate locations. PSCo should control the manufacturing and pricing, paying the licensee a commission on sales, or sell it directly to the licensee, maintaining a healthy margin, as in a franchise agreement. PSCo should market this under an appropriate brand name.

Other Considerations

The home office workers have distinctly different needs from the telecommuters. The telecommuters perceive that they have, or should have, a complete support system for working at home through their corporate connection. Their needs focus more on the products that will make life easier—for example, the surge protector with back-up power supply, the wall-size monitor, and the tiered or individual circuit UPS.

The individual, self-employed home office worker does not have a back-up support system, and therein lies a major opportunity to provide a "turnkey" support system for design, planning, equipment sales, instruction, service packages, and even emergency hot lines. Self-employed workers, too, desire back-up power supply, but their more immediate needs focus on getting started, and how to deal with the psychological impact of suddenly working at home.

Most home office workers want to maintain control over the equipment and software they need, but they need information as to what's available and, in many cases, supply sources.

The need for a uniform power supply is universal. Respondents have learned to expect power outages, but they need to "keep going" and, at a minimum, not lose their work. They expect back-up systems to last a minimum of five minutes, and ideally up to an hour.

The home office workers want a monthly payment plan when they buy high-end items, as cash flow and capital are critical issues for them. However, the telecommuter expects the company to pay for everything.

General Findings for Executives

Following are the general findings for the executives working within the target groups listed in the objectives section. In most cases the respondents were working in the human resources area, and in every case they have responsibility for evaluation of the telecommuting program, either established or potential.

In most cases, the decision-making process for a telecommuting program was employee centered. Most of the companies with active programs started telecommuting based on employee requests, centering on family considerations, e.g., children, spousal relocation, a desire to save commuting time, and even desires to be more productive due to a more "environmentally friendly" atmosphere.

Once the employee requests were registered, the human resources directors were expected to analyze the telecommuting opportunities based on more tangible, bottom-line considerations. These would include increased productivity, saving of office space, potential savings regarding benefits packages, even gaining public relations benefits from improving environmental conditions.

The driving force behind these considerations was the competitive activity they were sensing. The competitive threat is so strong they believe the only way they can compete is to stay "lean and mean" in the marketplace. They have restructured their departments to reflect this, and the restructuring has caused considerable angst among the employees.

Because of this, the prevailing feelings were that corporate cultures were all employee related, but this could be a bias due to the respondent pool, heavily human resources oriented. Most of the respondents reported on a management philosophy of keeping the employees secure and feeling positive about the organization, believing this would lead to increased productivity.

The other common issue was the need for innovation, for the rapid development and deployment of new products and services. They all recognize that their businesses should be customer driven, and they feel a need to establish a steady stream of new product development, and they are looking to their suppliers to help furnish this.

Companies with Telecommuters

Most executives at companies using telecommuters are at a loss as to how to evaluate the potential savings or effectiveness of a telecommuting program. They suspect it could be highly productive, but they don't know how to evaluate it to make proper recommendations. Only one respondent had made a specific proposal (ten years ago), which was rejected for lack of data.

In most all cases the existing telecommuting program was motivated by the employee for personal reasons (children, health, spousal relocation). No formal procedure is used to select telecommuters, and it is recognized that not all employees are "appropriate" for telecommuting, due to motivational factors.

All respondents with telecommuting programs report that the employee's immediate manager or supervisor made the decision to permit telecommuting, and they are the ones that judge the effectiveness of the telecommuter. The manager considers the employee motivation primarily, then the actual job function.

There is no consistent pattern regarding types of jobs, units, or departments allowing telecommuting. As it is employee driven, the supervisor makes the judgment as to whether the type of work can be done at home. A lot of clerical work is done at home, some graphics, and claims adjusters who must be in the field seem appropriate.

No firms used outside consultants to help establish a program, but most said they would have, had one been available.

There is a general recognition among all executives interviewed that telecommuting is the wave of the future, based on: increasing real estate costs, greater productivity of employees, increased employee morale, and family considerations.

In most cases the supervisor and the employee agree on goals, and productivity is measured against those goals. These are informal arrangements—formal contracts are not involved.

Most telecommuters work at home one or two days a week, and there is no consistent pattern as to which days. Scheduling is determined on a need basis. In some situations (claims adjusters, sales) employees will spend four to four and one-half days a week in the field, transmit data at the end of the day, then report to the office once a week for reviews, assignments, and other functions. Telecommuting is considered a permanent function, though flexible as to amount and schedules.

Only one telecommuting rotation pattern was discovered, that being with airline and travel representatives. They were rotated between a home office environment and the corporate office on a regular basis, at least every three months, to be updated with new fares, rates, and other rapidly changing data.

As most telecommuting has been employee driven, the employee already has computer hardware and software equipment. Often the equipment, particularly software, is not compatible with the main office, so the company will supply the necessary software. In some cases the company has supplied the hardware equipment, or is considering providing an allowance for the employee to buy the equipment.

The human resources directors report that managers of telecommuters are initially reluctant to allow telecommuting. The managers feel threatened by it, see it as a loss of control, and don't generally promote the concept. However, after trying it, they are more comfortable as they see improved productivity and morale.

With the federal government, all evaluations and decisions regarding telecommuting are made in Washington, D.C. by the heads of the individual agencies or departments. There are a few local telecommuters, particularly in the GSA, but that is strictly off the record! One division, the Department of Defense, has a pilot program in El Segundo, CA, but no one else is allowed telecommuters until the results are complete. The heads of each department in Washington evaluate and will make decisions on the telecommuting program.

There is a general dissatisfaction with the poor quality telephone service in some areas, and with inconsistent power supply. The telephone service is primarily faulted for long lead times for installation, and for poor quality transmission and reception, including static, low volume, and interrupted service.

The electrical supply is faulted by frequent power outages. This seems to occur in good weather, and in bad. The foothill areas, and the mountain areas from Evergreen to Bailey are purportedly "terrible service areas . . . with frequent outages and no back-up service available." Several employers reported such an intense dissatisfaction with "reliable power" that they were looking for alternative sources, including acquiring their own back-up generators in some areas with high density employee residents.

Companies without Telecommuters

Companies without telecommuters would like to have help evaluating a telecommuting program. They recognize the need, the trend, and the opportunity, but are immobilized due to lack of information or knowledge.

Decisions to begin a telecommuting program are left to the individual unit supervisors. As yet there is no widespread (company or department) evaluation, rather it is done on a case-by-case basis. Only a few companies have considered telecommuting programs on a formal basis, and in all but one case (Jones Cable), they have reviewed the merits of the program only because of employee requests. However, most acknowledge that they are currently, or soon will be, considering such programs.

All respondents said they would prefer to establish telecommuting rather than contract out work. Their employee retention is important, and their motivation is to keep an already trained employee (but realize we were interviewing human resources people—financial people may have a different perspective!).

Non-telecommuting companies recognize there are potential benefits to a program, including employee satisfaction, increased productivity, environmental issues, and potential office space savings.

Several respondents indicated a desire for some kind of program or software to help them evaluate whether an employee is suitable for telecommuting. We did not have a concept board on this, but our projective research techniques uncovered this need. They are looking for guidance as to how to evaluate when, if, and how they should approach consideration of a telecommuter program. When our boards suggested savings on real estate space, benefits, and increased productivity, it got their attention. They are really looking for a model to help them assess their needs and potential energy savings.

These respondents suspect certain job functions would be better suited to telecommuting than others. These would include clerical positions, some writing and document preparation, even graphics. However, jobs that require frequent interaction with other people, such as laboratory work, initial sales calls, and management briefings, would not immediately be identified as potentials for telecommuting assignments.

Evaluation of the productivity of a telecommuter would be left up to the supervisor, including setting goals and workload expectations.

It is anticipated that in the future the companies would help the telecommuters obtain state-of-the-art equipment. This would be by helping finance the equipment, and, in some cases, actually providing it for the employee.

Established benefits would be extended to the telecommuter, under existing benefits packages—e.g., health insurance, workers compensation—but the employee would be expected to provide liability insurance through homeowner policies.

Concepts for Customer Executives

Few differences were noted in the concept evaluation between companies with or without telecommuting programs. Executives in companies without programs tend to perceive a need for help in evaluating the opportunity for telecommuting, and executives in companies with telecommuting programs tended to express a need for support in evaluating the effectiveness of the program, and in product and software to support the employees. Specific concepts they wanted were as follows:

Surge Protector

Many executives related "horror" stories of employees losing material due to power outages. The surge protector concept was highly regarded, and needed immediately. The back-up need only be about five minutes, although some thought up to an hour would be better. They expected to pay from $50 to $200 for this unit, depending on the length of the back-up. This is seen as particularly important for remote sites. Several respondents thought the cords should be labeled for printer, FAX, phone, or computer, and stated there should be five or six cords.

Phone Number That Follows You Everywhere

A great idea that just keeps rising to the top is the phone number that "follows" the respondent. "A phenomenal idea—just do it!" This is seen as the answer to current customer service problems, as the provider can be reachable at any place, any time. However, it must be user friendly, as there are many complaints about voice mail. Several respondents wanted FAX service added to the concept, and an easy directional switch to direct calls as needed.

Help in Establishing and Monitoring Telecommuting Programs

There is an incredible need within companies with and without existing telecommuting programs for guidance in establishing, equipping, and monitoring telecommuting programs. This trend is so new that human resources people and their organizations are neither trained nor equipped to properly analyze the potential. These executives need a "turnkey" service to come to their environment, analyze their needs, recommend a program, then service the program from equipment to training.

They would expect to pay from $3,000 to $15,000 as a one-time consulting fee for this service, which they would like billed monthly, and would expect it to be provided by USWest or Public Service Company. Development of the software should be outsourced, and a consulting service retained to help PSCo develop expertise in design, needs assessment, and the other environmental factors. PSCo can market this under the H-O-W program, but aimed toward the executives. There should be a program for executives and a separate program for the worker, as needs are quite different. This can also be marketed effectively by a subsidiary organization with expertise in this area.

Help to Monitor the Productivity of Telecommuters

There is a pervasive need for help in monitoring the productivity of telecommuters, although supervisors are reluctant to acknowledge the need. Managers see the need, but the supervisors are reticent about admitting that they are in need of help in evaluating such a program, and they tend to establish programs to provide some form of evaluation, thereby finding ways to justify their decision to initiate a telecommuter program. There is some skepticism that the program would work as well as presented, but it is seen as needed, and very valuable if it can work this way. This should be outsourced for development, then marketed as part of the PSCo executive telecommuter program. Direct marketing nationally should be considered.

Satellite Meeting Rooms

The concept of satellite meeting rooms continues to gain strength, and is closely associated with Public Service Company or USWest. Executives see a real need for this, more for a work center than for a meeting room. They feel we should put an office where the employees are, rather than the reverse. Apparently NEC Tokyo is doing this, with success, and the general feeling is that it should be done here. These would be in strip malls, shopping malls, restaurants, and copy centers.

Consulting Services for Telecommuters

Again, we see the need for a consulting service for the employees to help them establish a home office program, and to help the family adjust to it. Moving into a telecommuting environment is traumatic for most, and there is a perceived need for a turnkey consulting service to help ease the transition. The respondents believe the employer should provide this upon initiation of a telecommuting program. Most executives said they would happily pay for such a service, and would expect to pay from $1,000 to $3,000 per employee. They would expect this on a contract basis, and would expect the service to be offered by USWest, Public Service Company, or a private consulting group. This service should be developed and marketed by PSCo.

Concepts Recommended for Development

Following the above analysis we prepared a screening model to select the concepts that have shown consistent strength throughout the project. We utilized the following criteria for our development decisions:

1. Relative subjective appeal among focus group respondents and executives during the interviews

2. Ease of entry into the marketplace: available channels of distribution and awareness of need by end-users

3. Potential market size (based on PSCo selling price to channels of distribution)

4. Growth potential

5. Available technology

6. Ability of PSCo to develop the concept internally

7. Ease of outsourcing

8. Number of mentions by respondents as a projection of a product/service they'd most like to have, when forced to discriminate among all concepts

Potential market size has been calculated on known data, on the prices respondents said they would be willing to pay or prices of similar competitive products, and conservative, educated guesses at potential share or penetration rates. The known data used in the following calculations include the following:

- There are 40 million home office workers in the United States, projected to 45 million by 1996 (PSCo).

- There are 58 million households in the United States with incomes over $25,000 per year, 650,000 in Colorado (Census).

- Penetration of computers was 39 percent of U.S. households in 1994, projected to 45 percent in 1995 (CACI), therefore about 45 million households in 1995.

- There were 24 million cellular phones registered in 1994, projected to over 25 million in 1995 (FCC), with estimates of 350,000 in Colorado.

- There will be 13 million telecommuters by 1998 (Link).

- There were 1,333,700 new construction units in the United States in 1994, and about 16,000 in Colorado (PSCo).

- Colorado accounts for about 1.5 percent of the total U.S. population, or 1.5 million households.

- Colorado is assumed to have a household computer penetration of 50 percent, or 750,000 computer households.

PSCo has the capability, and the interest, in marketing these products and services nationally, and licensing agreements and marketing teams are being assembled to launch regional and national programs. The project was considered highly successful, as the Perception Expansion Theory resulted in identifying several major new product opportunities.

References

Asker, D. A., and Kevin Lane Keller (1989), "Consumer Evaluations of Brand Extensions," *Journal of Marketing* 54 (January 1990), pp. 27–41.

Anderson, N. H., *Information Integration Theory: A Case History in Experimental Science,* Vol, 1 (New York: Academic Press, 1982).

Bittner, John R., *Mass Communication,* 6th ed. (Boston: Allyn and Bacon, 1996).

Black, Jay, and Jennings Bryant, *Introduction to Media Communication,* 4th ed. (Dubuque, IA: Brown and Benchmark Publishers, 1995).

Bovee, Courtland L., John V. Thill, George P. Dovel, and Marian Burk Wood, *Advertising Excellence* (New York: McGraw-Hill, 1995).

Clement, Mary, and Werner Grotemeyer, "The Iterative Positioning Process: An International Approach from the Pharmaceutical Industry," *Marketing and Research Today* 18, No. 2 (1990): pp. 85–96.

Conover, Theodore E., *Graphic Communications Today* (New York: West Publishing Company, 1995).

DeFleur, Melvin L., and Everette E. Dennis, *Understanding Mass Communication: A Liberal Arts Perspective* (Boston: Houghton Mifflin Company, 1996).

Dominick, Joseph R., *The Dynamics of Mass Communication* (New York: McGraw-Hill, Inc., 1994).

Farrar, Ronald T., *Mass Communication: An Introduction to the Field,* 2nd ed. (Dubuque, IA: Brown and Benchmark Publishers, 1996).

Fishbein, Martin, "Attitudes and the Prediction of Behavior," in M. Fishbein, ed. *Readings in Attitude Theory and Measurement* (New York: John Wiley, 1976), pp. 477–492.

Fishbein, M., and I. Ajzen, *Belief, Attitude, Intention and Behavior: An Introduction to Theory and Research* (Reading, MA: Addison-Wesley, 1975).

Fisher, B. Aubrey, *Perspectives on Human Communication* (New York: Macmillan Publishing Co., Inc., 1978).

Fisher, Marsh, *The IdeaFisher* (Princeton: Peterson's/Pacesetter Books, 1996).

Gardner, Meryl P., "Does Attitude toward the Ad Affect Brand Attitudes Under a Brand Evaluation Set?" *Journal of Marketing Research* 22 (1985): pp. 192–198.

Gruenwald, George, *New Product Development: What Really Works* (Lincolnwood, IL: NTC Business Books, 1985).

Haskins, Jack, and Alice Kendrik, *Successful Advertising Research Methods* (Lincolnwood, IL: NTC Business Books, 1993).

Hurlburt, Allen, *The Design Concept* (New York: Watson-Guptill Publications, 1981).

Katz, Daniel, "The Functional Approach to the Study of Attitudes," *Public Opinion Quarterly* 24 (1960): pp. 163–204.

Lewin, Miriam, *Understanding Psychological Research* (New York, John Wiley and Sons, 1979).

Lutz, Richard J., "A Functional Approach to Consumer Attitude Research," in H. K. Hunt, ed., *Advances in Consumer Research*, Vol. V (Ann Arbor, MI: Association for Consumer Research, 1978): pp. 360–369.

Marra, James L., *Advertising Creativity: Techniques for Generating Ideas* (Englewood Cliffs, NJ: Prentice Hall, 1990).

Marra, James L., *Advertising Copywriting: Techniques for Improving Your Skills* (Englewood Cliffs, NJ: Prentice Hall, 1993).

McLuhan, Marshall, "From Counterblast," *Mass Media: Forces in Society* (Chicago: Harcourt Brace Jovanovich, 1972).

McGuire, William J., "The Nature of Attitudes and Attitude Change," in G. Lindzey and E. Aronson, eds. *Handbook of Social Psychology*, 2nd ed. Vol. 3 (Reading, MA: Addison-Wesley, 1973), pp. 136–154.

McGuire, William J., "The Probabilogical Model of Cognitive Structure and Attitude Change," in R. E. Petty, T. M. Ostrom, and T. C. Brock, eds., *Cognition Responses in Persuasion* (Hillsdale, NJ: Erlbaum, 1981).

McQuail, Denis, *Mass Communication Theory: An Introduction* (Thousand Oaks: Sage Publications, 1994).

Miller, Gerald R., *Speech Communication, a Behavioral Approach* (New York: The Bobbs-Merrill Co., 1978).

Mittal, Banwari, "The Relative Roles of Brand Beliefs and Attitude toward the Ad as Mediators of Brand Attitude: A Second Look," *Journal of Marketing Research* XXVII (1990): pp. 209–219.

Neuliep, James W., *Human Communication Theory: Applications and Case Studies* (Boston: Allyn and Bacon, 1996).

Patrick, Gerald L., "Identification of Industrial New Product Opportunities through Utilization of Graphic Stimuli," New Product Development: E.S.O.M.A.R. (Barcelona, Spain: E.S.O.M.A.R., 1990).

Patrick, Gerald L., "How to Identify Needs and Adapt American New Product Concepts for Successful Marketing in Europe: A Case Study," Marketing Strategies in a Changing World: E.S.O.M.A.R. (Luxembourg, Belgium: E.S.O.M.A.R., 1991).

Pfau, Michael, and Roxanne Parrott, *Persuasive Communication Campaigns* (Boston: Allyn and Bacon, 1993).

Reeves, Rosser, *Reality in Advertising* (New York: Knopf, 1968).

Reis, Al, and Jack Trout, *Positioning: The Battle for Your Mind* (New York: Warner Books, 1981).

Rokeach, M., *The Nature of Human Values* (New York: Free Press, 1973).

Rosenberg, M., and C. Hovland, eds., *Attitude, Organization and Change* (New Haven: Yale University Press, 1960).

Russell, J. Thomas, and W. Ronald Lane, *Kleppner's Advertising Procedure*, 13th ed. (Englewood Cliffs, NJ: Prentice Hall, 1996).

Sandage, C. H., Vernon Fryburger, and Kim Rotzoll, *Advertising Theory and Practice* (New York: Longman, Inc., 1989), p. 125.

Schiffman, Leon G. and Leslie Lazar Kanuk, *Consumer Behavior* (Englewood Cliffs, NJ: Prentice-Hall, 1978).

Schultz, Don E., Dennis Martin, and William P. Brown, *Strategic Advertising Campaigns*, 2nd ed. (Chicago: Crain Books, 1984).

Simmons, Robert E., *Communication Campaign Management: A Systems Approach* (New York: Longman, 1990).

Tuncalp, Cecil, and J. N. Sheth, "Prediction of Attitudes: A Comparative Study of the Rosenberg, Fishbein and Sheth Models," *Journal of Marketing Research* 22 (1985): pp. 389–404.

U.S. Bureau of Labor Statistics, Bulletin 2307 (Washington, DC: U.S. Government Printing Office, 1994).

Vivian, John, *The Media of Mass Communication*, 3rd ed. (Boston: Allyn and Bacon, 1995).

Weimer, Walter B., "Communication, Speech, and Psychological Models of Man: Review and Commentary" *Communication Yearbook 2* (1978).

Wells, William, John Burnett, and Sandra Moriarty, *Advertising Principles and Practice*, 3rd ed. (Englewood Cliffs, NJ: Prentice Hall, 1995).

Weyer, Robert S., Jr., *Cognitive Organization and Change: An Information Processing Approach* (New York: Lawrence Erlbaum Associates, 1974).

Wilson, Stan Le Roy, *Mass Media/Mass Culture* (New York: McGraw-Hill, Inc., 1994).

INDEX

V

VALS. *See* Values and Lifestyles System (VALS)
Value (financial), addition of perceived, 102
Value-added concepts
building, 101–110
tips for successful strategy, 108–109
Values (philosophical)
attitudes and, 55
defined, 56–57
hierarchy of, 29
Values and Lifestyles System (VALS), 80–81, 136–138
Volkswagen, 87–88
ad for, 92
Volvo, ad for, 94

W

Wave series ideation, 128–129
Weimer, Walter B., 42, 55
Wells, Mary, 102
Wells, William, 131
Wells Rich Green, Inc., 102
W.I.I.F.M. (What's In It for Me?), 65–66
Women. *See* Gender
World Wide Web, 157
Worries, 81
Writing. *See* Copywriting
WWW. *See* World Wide Web

X

Xerox, 27

Y

Yankelovich Monitor, 138–144